As Good As It Gets
The Story of St Helens' Grand Slam Class of 2006

Mike Critchley

Vertical Editions
www.verticaleditions.com

First published in the United Kingdom in 2014 by Vertical Editions, Unit 4a, Snaygill Industrial Estate, Skipton, North Yorkshire BD23 2QR

www.verticaleditions.com

ISBN 978-1-904091-86-8

A CIP catalogue record for this book is available from the British Library

Cover design by HBA, York

Printed and bound by CMP (uk) Ltd, Poole, Dorset

For my wife Kate and daughter Rosa, who both
helped make 2006 so extra special.

Contents

Acknowledgements

The writing of this book would not have been possible without the co-operation of coach Daniel Anderson, who was always ready to give me his time, opinion, guidance and insight during the course of the 2006 and, indeed, throughout his time at the Saints.

His retrospective input to the book, gleaned from meeting me during his stay in St Helens for the 2013 Rugby League World Cup, was also invaluable.

Plenty of others gave up their time to help too, most notably Paul Wellens, Jon Wilkin, Ade Gardner, James Roby and Apollo Perelini.

A massive thank you goes to club photographer Bernard Platt for providing such fantastically striking images both on the pitch and behind scenes.

Thanks also to Alex Service for checking the stats; Alan Turner for hosting many a post match discussion at the George; Dave Davies for his wit and wisdom on away days; prolific ghost writer Andrew Quirke for his marketing tips; Paul and Julie Devanney and Paul Dixon for their post-match company over a pint; and Saints tireless press officer Mike Appleton for his assistance on this project.

Additionally I'd like to thank Saints chairman Eamonn McManus for having the vision, and the chequebook, to back Daniel's judgement and help build a team that put a smile on the face of our town and create so many happy memories.

Introduction

"2006? Was that the year Saints won Eurovision, Crufts and the Chelsea Flower Show?"

"Yep, that's the one."

So went the conversation with one of my mates in the Phoenix after explaining that I was putting the finishing touches to this manuscript. It said it all about how utterly dominant Daniel Anderson's class of 2006 had been. They took out every pot and award available, both team and individual and only lost four games during the course of a gruelling 35 match season. Even in defeat the deficits were a mere 2, 1, 2 and 4, the latter being conceded by a team packed with juniors in Catalan. To underline their superiority, to write a postscript to 2006, in the subsequent World Club Challenge at Bolton they saw off Wayne Bennett's Brisbane Broncos featuring Darren Lockyer, Darius Boyd and Petero Civoniceva the following February.

Any conversation about the 2006 season invariably switches immediately to the sublime skills of ace Australian centre Jamie Lyon; the man with that magic ingredient, that special X-Factor, his swivel of the hips, step and then the flicking out of an audacious offload to a grateful Ade Gardner. But the achievements of Daniel Anderson's class of 2006 were about much more than the classy contribution from the Saints' second Wizard of Aus.

There are so many other iconic images from that campaign still so vividly engrained on the memory. Take Jon Wilkin, sporting a bandage to stem the bloodflow from a badly broken nose, blowing a kiss to the crowd after scoring his second try in the Challenge Cup Final win.

Or Paul Anderson providing the coup de grace against Leeds by calmly hoofing over a touchline conversion, turning round to see the Popular Side going absolutely doolally.

And how many snapshots of sheer brilliance did Sean Long provide, particularly in his dominant cup final display which saw him take out the Lance Todd Trophy for a record breaking third time.

Ade Gardner had a wow of a season in 2006, and his spring-heeled attack of Long's crossfield kick to collect and touch down to help clinch the title underlined that perfectly.

And who could forget Vinnie Anderson creasing Wigan's Danny Tickle in half with that thunderous tackle, and then stand over him triumphant like a victorious gladiator; great imagery from an outstanding year of achievement for the men in the red vee.

It was a year that spoilt Saints fans rotten, and just to cap it all Joe Public voted them BBC Sports Personality team of the year to howls of anguish from middle England. It certainly put St Helens on the map, and underlined what the town continues to be really good at – producing and nurturing world class rugby league footballers. The playing fields of Blackbrook, Portico, Clock Face, Thatto Heath, Haydock, Bold, Haresfinch and Pilkingtons have provided a steady stream of players to the pro game. Admittedly, the Saints club have always cast their net even wider, regularly trawling the world to bring in key players to complement those homespun stars. And so they did in 2006 with a melting pot of Samoans, Kiwis, Aussies and Tykes, combining with born and bred Sintelliners to stunning effect.

Maybe we should have known that it was going to be a blinding season – the year did end with a lucky number six after all. A casual look down the St Helens RFC's honours board reveal that Saints had truly discovered the joys of six. The club's first ever Challenge Cup Final win came in 1956 and ten years later Alex Murphy skippered that illustrious four-cups team to Wembley success over Wigan. In 1976 Kel Coslett climbed the steps beneath the Twin Towers to collect that most ornate of trophies from Maggie Thatcher after the team dubbed Dad's Army had seen off holders and favourites Widnes.

And of course in 1996 Bobbie Goulding bombed the hapless

Nathan Graham and the Bulls into submission to win the trophy back in a year in which Saints also took out the inaugural Super League crown. The only blip in the pattern was 1986, but the eighties were a write-off decade generally.

The class of 2006 was arguably the most effective and clinical playing machine ever assembled under the eyes of the salary cap monitors. On and off the field, the club had strengths everywhere and was one at ease with itself, with all pulling in the same direction, starting with the chairman. Eamonn McManus backed the coach's judgement and paid for Daniel Anderson's shopping bill – bringing in the players to execute the master plan. Obviously, Anderson had to coach them – and manage those big egos and huge characters – but he did so masterfully. With skipper Paul Sculthorpe plagued with a knee injury for most of the year, Anderson placed a lot of faith in two players of rare talent – Keiron Cunningham and Sean Long, and that pair repaid him in spades in 2006.

Those players, of course, thrived behind the most dominant front row unit ever assembled in Super League – a phalanx of forwards arguably even more awesome than the one Paul Anderson had featured in during his long spell at Bradford Bulls in the early noughties.

St Helens fans will always list their favourite teams and their best year for standing on the Knowsley Road terraces. Older supporters will throw out the late 50s and early 60s team of Voll, Vinty, Huddart and Murph. Or maybe the 1966 one that collected the Championship, Challenge Cup, League Leaders and Lancashire League.

Others will select the 1976 crop, particularly as it was the last hurrah from that ageing team of greats before the club's 20 year spell living in the shadows of others. Shaun McRae's 96 double winners tick so many boxes – both in terms of pure entertainment value and because of the joy and relief of taking out the two big prizes for the first time in two decades. A few, too, will nod towards the Grand Final winning teams of 2000 and 2002.

This book is a celebration of the achievements of 2006 and it draws on reports and interviews I conducted with the coach and players at the time, intertwined with retrospective reflection pieces

10

carried out some seven or eight years later with those involved in that momentous season.

It is dedicated to all those players, coaches and spectators who were in that number when the Saints went marching in.

1

The Team that Daniel Built

When Saints coach Daniel Anderson left St Helens to return to his native Sydney the week after the 2008 Grand Final defeat it closed a chapter on one of the most glorious spells of the club's history. The masterful, but likeable Australian's three-and-a-year tenure of office had seen gallons of Brasso required in the trophy room – but apart from the annual harvest of cups and shields, his input into the running of the club was immeasurable.

It could have all been so different and initially Ian Millward's dismissal provoked uproar – Basil, for all his quirks and scrapes over the years, had been popular with the supporters. During the Challenge Cup game against York, Saints' first since the sacking and barely a couple weeks before Anderson's arrival in May 2005, irate fans stormed the main stand brandishing hurriedly photocopied pictures of his fallen predecessor. Raucous choruses of "Ian Millward's Barmy Army!" and "Sack the board! Sack the board!" rang out around the ground.

Millward was sacked for gross misconduct after the club's management had totted up his verbal abuse of Warrington press officer Gina Coldrick, his swearing at a Rugby League official during a match and his admonishment of St Helens press officer Alex Turner, after he had let Wigan player Brian Carney come into the stadium to film while the team were training. Given that swearing was such a part and parcel of the game, a lot of fans thought 'so what!' This was after all Ian Millward who, after seeing Darren Britt suffer a broken cheekbone in the bruising 2003 game against Hull, had used 31 swear words in the press conference – culminating in saying that his injured players "are all fucked!"

The club was ill at ease with itself after the dismissal and if ever there was a need to find a new coach to pour oil on troubled waters this was the time. Enter Daniel Anderson – much less well known than namesake Chris – but a coach who simply got on with the job.

The anger soon dissipated when Saints started winning again and a lot of those angry fans soon changed their tune when Millward was lured over the other side of Billinge Lump to join the Warriors. If – and it is a big 'if' – the Wigan board thought they would be rubbing salt in an open Saints wound by recruiting Millward then it backfired badly. If anything it took the 'Bring Back Basil brigade' out of the equation and allowed new boss Daniel Anderson to calmly pour soothing balm on any remaining wounds created from that painful separation.

But when he arrived in May 2005 the landscape was still quite rocky, particularly with the aggrieved Millward still on the prowl like a lion with a thorn in his paw and intent on regaining his kingdom. Those noises off stage did not affect Anderson's outlook, although he did initially say that he was surprised and felt very lucky to be in St Helens. The rest of it, the worries whether the fans would take to him or their pining for his predecessor, did not register. It certainly did not give the new boss any sleepless nights.

"I didn't care – it had nothing to do with me. All I felt was I had to get the respect of the players first. Once I had got that I knew it would not be hard for respect of fans to follow – because I knew if the players were playing good footy then the fans would recognise that.

"People have a good grasp and know if you are an honest, genuine character; they can pick up on the subtleties. I knew if I just behaved like myself, and carried that character through and not let myself be whimsical, I knew I would have an opportunity to get some success," Anderson said.

Having been in England with the 2004 Kiwi tourists, Anderson said he appreciated the knowledge and passion of the spectators and always harboured the ambition to coach over here and so was pleased to get a shout from Eamonn McManus.

For the chairman making the decision – after sacking the popular Millward – it was a call that probably weighed heavier on his shoulders. But Anderson repaid the faith in him in spades.

It soon became fairly obvious that Saints' defence was going to be the first thing to get the Daniel Anderson treatment. That was certainly something for him to get stuck into given Saints' deep-seated philosophy that developed under Millward was tilted towards a swashbuckling style of attack. There was a carefree approach of 'if they score 30, we'll score 40'. That soon went with the desire to put on big hits and keep the line intact becoming as insatiable as running in a length of field score.

Anderson explained: "The main thing I knew I could work on was defence, because that was my speciality. I worked hard on the defensive systems in the first six months. The best way to look at my 120 odd games at Saints is to look at points against and I think we have averaged about 15. If you can have that over a three-and-a-half year period you are going to win a lot of games.

"That is impressive. I have always thought defence is under-applauded – everyone, including myself, loves a try, but there were some players in this team that love defence and maybe they did feel as rewarded as some of our attacking players. Keiron is the key here – he is good at attack, but he has a real passion for defence. To see big tackles and defensive play held up in the same esteem as a try encouraged everyone to say 'well I don't mind tackling either'. It becomes pretty infectious."

Full-back Paul Wellens, who was charged with organising that defence, very quickly noticed the change in style and substance from the old regime to the new one.

He said: "When Daniel first came to the club in 2005 he inherited a side that under Ian Millward had always been attack minded. There were plenty of 32-28 sorts of games and we could also blow out a few scorelines too.

"When Daniel came his first two or three days were defence, defence, defence! And the change in us was noticeable almost instantaneously. He'd say 'try doing this, try that' and all of a sudden we were defending like a different team almost overnight. It was remarkable.

"It struck me that if we started defending, given we could still score points for fun, we were going to win the majority of our rugby games. A lot of people talk about the attacking flair that we had but a lot of the success that we had was built on our defence."

It was not simply about tackle bags, white boards, flip charts and defensive drills, there were other attitudes and outlooks of the Saints coach that were soon picked up on by those working with and under him. The club's strength and conditioning coach Apollo Perelini has always been an astute judge of character and he was very quickly on the new boss's wavelength and got used to his personal traits.

"Daniel has great philosophies – all he wanted was for a player to have a good attitude towards training, be willing to have the work ethic and get down and do what needed to be done," Perelini said.

"He was a hard task master and he wanted to do his best for the team and also the players. He knew their different personalities and knew how to tap into each player and we worked together as a team to get the best out of each other. It worked really well.

"The most important thing with Daniel was getting players to play for each other and do things which were selfless that would benefit the team. He instilled a good mental toughness in there but also a lot of respect. That was a two-way street – older blokes having respect for the younger guys and vice versa. He created a culture at training and that was turn up to do the job.

"Daniel had two hats – the hard general, tough task master, old school teacher hat – but also, the 'I am your mate, you can talk to me'. It made him very approachable."

Anderson's way of finding a way through to different players probably dipped into the psychology he needed to get into the minds of children who had not done their algebra homework. He could be good cop and bad cop within the same dressing room.

Paul Wellens noticed that approach and recalls with a smile how Anderson used, when required, different voices when dealing with different players, but to achieve the same objective.

"Whereas on one occasion he gave Leon the hairdryer treatment with Maurie he would call him Malama, the name of his son who was just two or three at the time. He'd say 'how

15

are you going Malama?' It would imply Maurie was playing like a toddler – and you could see it getting through to Maurie to the extent that it would fire him up to go out there and tear shreds off the opposition. It was a new way of saying 'up your game'."

It got results. In a year when it was always going to be hard accommodating everyone in the 17, he was able to rotate in a manner that freshened-up the squad and kept others on their toes. There was also a rapid advancement of some of the younger players – the two young Blackbrook Jameses, Ade Gardner, Jon Wilkin and Maurie Fa'asavalu.

Anderson explained: "We had a quorum of very good senior players, it was easy to work with the young players coming through because we knew they were so talented. We knew there were plenty of things to do to improve Ade and Wilko, then there was Robes and Jammer. I had seen James Graham as a junior and watched him on tape. The week I arrived he started playing first grade regularly and I don't think he ever played reserve grade since.

"Most of those things were about giving them more confidence – I didn't tell them how to play rugby league. It was a case of giving them a bit of support to allow them do their own thing, they were late teenagers or early 20s sometimes you just have to let the chain out. They made some mistakes but that was the character of players to learn from those mistakes.

"I am very hard on young players as anyone, but if you can mould the plasticine of a young player, you will get the rewards down the track. What we try to do is shape them and give players expertise and ways to improve, but in the end it is down to their own natural ability and competitive nature that comes through.

"I am not as hard on senior players, what I learned at St Helens, which I never had before, is to build relationships and get the best out of the senior players and big stars. I always had a great affinity with junior developing players and young first graders on the edge of representative football. I was able to add the string to my bow of getting the best out of seasoned players, Baloo, Keiron and Longy – that ilk of 30-plus player. Extracting everything you can out of them using different training techniques.

"I still had to talk technically to Longy and Keiron but they were already world class decision makers. Keiron is one of the best decision makers I have ever seen."

Having now experienced working under six club coaches and three at international level Wilkin, who was only 22 at the time of those tumultuous triumphs of that year, can now give an informed appreciation on Anderson's methods.

He said: "Our training at the time was very repetitive, we were well drilled and would complain, but if you understand Daniel's background as a teacher he essentially devised a curriculum and the things that were important to him were drilled home to us. In a way we were revising for our exams every week. We knew what the questions would be, on a match day, and our training reflected that."

It was not simply about the individuals – it was a system that worked even on the rare occasion when there was wholesale changes, like when a mixed team of young debutants and a smattering of old heads were sent to play Catalan Dragons. Those stand-ins bought into the whole ethos of pride and responsibility and were 60 seconds away from pulling it off.

For the players, Anderson did not turn the art of coaching or simply following his instructions into a complex rocket science, but accountability was important.

Wellens said: "Daniel really kept things very simple. It was basically a case of 'this is your job', or 'you do that and we will be fine'. It was the case that every single player knew what their role was – there was accountability. There was never a case in a game or in training where a player could say – 'ah but he should have done this'. Daniel would say, 'no, you should have been there'. He had that authority and so everyone had a role and there was no confusion in the group as to what needed doing."

It worked. And the trophy harvest that Saints reaped in 2006 was, among other things, testament to that. He was lucky that he had an extremely talented roster of players – but those big characters had to be directed and many of the big egos had to be managed. Anderson was not fazed by that – it was his job. And after each good win, trophy success or thrilling spectacle there was always a measured smile of satisfaction – no showboating, running on the pitch to leap on to players' backs, and to the Popular Side's disquiet on occasion, no response to "Daniel, Daniel, give us a wave!" Ironically, there was nothing of the sort of theatre and heart-on-the sleeve emotion that made predecessor Millward so popular with the fans and look like 'one of us'.

Anderson, however, never came across as aloof, he just quietly and conscientiously got on with the job, looking cool, calm and collected with his shades perched on his head as he gazed from his seat in the main stand. And he was always quick to share the credit throughout the organisation. No week went by without him mentioning in his weekly column in the *St Helens Star* someone who had made a positive input to the club's well being. One week he even thanked his hairdresser Christopher Bacon. And plaudits were dished out too within the organisation – whether it was praising chairman Eamonn McManus for recruitment or the work of the physios making sure there were always 17 bodies at the peak of fitness.

When Anderson finally left, of his own volition and time of choosing, he had guided the side to the top of Super League for four years on the trot, brought home three Challenge Cups, one World Club Championship and one Super League title.

He was, however, keen to share the credit for that silverware haul throughout the organisation. Anderson said: "The success at St Helens is a credit to the club and its culture. It is the players that do the business but we have very talented staff. I never sat on the shoulders of staff or players. If there's one thing I learned at St Helens it is to let people exhibit their own abilities. We had a very good physios department in Matty Viljoen and Joey Hayes, first class doctors and a variety of assistant coaches with plenty of assets. And added to that, I also had a good backroom staff including kitman Alan Clarke and match day manager Kel Coslett. They are all good characters and good men, too.

"But ultimately the winning of the games came from the single bloody mindedness and honesty of the players to do what they can."

2

Unfinished Business 2005

One ugly Friday night in Wigan is unwittingly the starting point of a journey which saw Saints create a virtually invincible playing machine; a team which combined steel, determination and flair with a confidence bordering on arrogance running through it. It did not happen in a way that anybody wanted and the events of September 9, 2005 left some pretty deep physical scars, but the consequences of that fateful evening also gave the men in the red vee ample motivation in the months that followed.

Earlier that year the Saints board had taken a shock decision, bordering on the unbelievable, to sack the coach that helped guide them to two title successes and a pair of Challenge Cup wins. Ian Millward had been dismissed, not for poor team performances, but for misconduct involving swearing at two press officers and an RFL match official. There was a bit of a kerfuffle at first but once the dust settled and new man Daniel Anderson installed at the helm, Saints rattled through 2005, handing Millward's Wigan a 75-0 thrashing in the Challenge Cup. It was a win that ultimately meant nothing as the men in the red vee subsequently came unstuck in a shock semi-final defeat by eventual winners Hull FC. That defeat was a blip – albeit a very costly one – in the course of a year which saw Saints rightly elevated to the top of the pile.

And so it was on to the JJB Stadium, as it was then named, where a Saints victory would seal the League Leaders' Shield. Remarkably Saints were also looking at ending a run of 11 successive losses at that ground dating back to September 2000. Ahead of the game Saints boss Anderson said: "I would like to think that those incentives are not our sole motivating factors, currently we have a mindset where we just want to play well for each other and be proud in our performances for the club.

"Six or seven weeks ago we said we want to win every game for the rest of the year and our goal has not changed.

"Saints are fortunate at present to have a large number of key personnel such as Sean Long, Keiron Cunningham, Paul Wellens and Jason Hooper feeling very fresh in mind and body. It is these four along with senior players Darren Albert and Paul Anderson who are leading our team each week."

Alas, those "fresh in mind and body" words would come back to haunt the Saints boss, for despite winning 38-12 it was at significant cost, with injuries sustained by Lee Gilmour, Sean Long and Darren Albert meaning that the army of Saints fans trudged out with feelings of anger and concern rather than jubilation at 'beating the pie-eaters'. What made matters worse was the fact that two of those injuries were caused by blatant acts of thuggery from Great Britain hooker Terry Newton. And had referee Ian Smith taken stronger action against Newton when he pole-axed Gilmour with a forearm across the face halfway through the first half, Long would not have been robbed of his chance of playing in another Grand Final. Sadly the first incident, which resulted in a distressed Gilmour leaving the field in a neck brace and on a stretcher, was placed on report leaving Newton free to clobber Long with a late, high tackle, shattering his cheekbone.

Newton was hit with a ten-match ban and £600 fine – but that was cold comfort to those injured players and the rest of the squad who would have to soldier on without them for the real crunch games of the season. Despite Albert's broken cheekbone, sustained in an accidental collision with Brett Dallas, meaning the Aussie had played his last game for Saints, and Long's face being smashed, there was no sign of any towels being thrown in by coach Anderson. There was no white flag being hoisted from the Knowsley Road turrets.

Later that week, after surveying the medical reports, Anderson declared: "The guys here are shattered by the news because they are both popular team members and outstanding players as well. Although their loss puts a dent in our aspirations, we are still committed to the cause.

"It hurts because those two players have contributed so much to our campaign to get into the play-offs this year. All players want to play in those big games and they make those contributions week-in and week-out to get the opportunities at the end of the year. Darren has lost his chance through an accident and Sean's has been robbed from him by foul play – it is bitterly disappointing.

"We will not allow those negatives to feed into our camp as we approach this crucial stage of the season. We will continue to play and work in a selfless manner and we have a number of players who are both talented and in form, and also a number of very committed rugby league players around them."

Saints tackled runners-up Leeds in the first play-off game of 2005 – a game in which a Jamie Lyon-inspired rally was too little, too late to make their first bite of the Old Trafford cherry count. Trailing 19-0, with makeshift duo Jon Wilkin and Jason Hooper operating at half back, Saints looked dead and buried until the Aussie whirlwind struck with 11 minutes remaining on the clock.

Using strength, nifty footwork and vision the Australian Test centre took the Leeds left hand side to the cleaners in a blistering six minute spell. Although Saints still fell short, that late defiance raised the crowd's morale and gave the team hope for the following week's last chance saloon tussle against the Bulls.

Alas, it was not to be. History books will show that Saints were eliminated 18-23 from the 2005 play-off series by the Bulls, therefore becoming the first Super League leaders not to make the Grand Final. However, those bald facts will not do justice to what was a mighty effort from the patched-up Saints in an utterly compelling blood and thunder encounter. Both sides left the field physically and mentally shattered after matching each other blow for blow during the full course of the 80 minutes.

Afterwards Bulls coach Brian Noble compared it to a tennis match, particularly a 17 minute spell when the ball did not go out of play as each took it in turns to make the other side blink first. With the scores locked at 18-all it became Ali v Frazier and McEnroe v Borg rolled into one.

Speaking three days later, reflecting on the season ending in defeat Anderson said: "Our players were very committed and competitive and threw everything into it, as did Bradford. We stuck to our game plan and were rewarded with a couple of opportunities, which we will be thinking about for a long time. We gave it everything, but we were out on our feet at the end – as were Bradford.

"Ultimately, the difference between the sides was Bradford got the ball to the right people at the right time and they did their job. Although it hurts to lose, character in this game is built more by adversity than it is by glory. We have lost three big games this year and two of them were at home.

"I am aware of that as a coach – you take it on the chin, but invariably we will learn from it. Some of these boys are going to play in more big games in the future and will have a better awareness of how it is going to go."

How prophetic those words would be. Some eight years later, reflecting on the end of that first campaign at Knowsley Road, Anderson admitted that the events of that year did indeed provide ample motivation to right a few injustices and to correct some deficiencies, even from the coaching staff, that had reared their head in 2005.

Anderson said: "I considered ourselves to be a little unlucky at the end of 2005.

"Admittedly, I was a little bit under-prepared and I had under-estimated the Challenge Cup and that semi-final loss against Hull FC had as much to do with me as it did any of the performances on the field.

"Then we still put it right after that in the Super League, and were still cruising but then came the Wigan away game where we lost all those players. We were flying until we lost those key personnel. I remember when we played at home against Bradford Bulls, when they knocked us out. We were pretty awesome that night considering we had so many players playing out of position, so many unusual players in various spots on the field, with Scott Moore and Jon Wilkin in the halves.

"It hurt us losing seasoned players like Albie and Longy, meaning we had to throw kids into key positions. For us to go as close as we did was outstanding. It was unfortunate and a little bit unlucky what had happened to us at the end of the year, and we felt a bit cheated because they were not normal injuries, they were sustained through foul play."

3

Key Jigsaw Pieces – Meli, Cayless, Pryce and Wilson

December is a time of hope, optimism, hard work, punishingly cold Taylor Park hill runs and sweaty gyms. And at the end of 2005 it was a time for some of Saints' new boys – on and off the pitch – to settle into new roles and surroundings. The weather was at its most inhospitable for the club's newest recruits from the NRL, with coach Daniel Anderson revealing that prop Jason Cayless and big Francis Meli enjoyed a new experience in their first week – training in the snow. As harsh a baptism as that was the Saints boss felt the two would benefit in the long run – and was under no illusions what his first new arrivals were going to bring to the party in 2006.

"Although the conditions are quite brutal at the moment it will be better for Francis and Jason in the long term as the conditions improve – they will appreciate that as the season progresses. Both are big guys with plenty of attributes to offer our side.

"Jason is a very tall man at 6ft 5in, but also has a big engine and is very quick for a prop. He is a tradesman front row forward, not a converted second rower, and joins the out and out experienced props we already have in Nick Fozzard and Paul Anderson.

"Young James Graham and Maurie Fa'asavalu are still learning their trade, but they are both developing well. Francis Meli may not be as quick as Darren Albert – not many wingers are – but you don't get to score 25 tries in the NRL by being a slouch. His support play and anticipation are tremendous and we are looking forward to him pulling on a Saints jersey."

The fleet-footed Albert had become a real crowd favourite –

after all, from Vollenhoven to Sullivan, there is nothing that a Knowsley Road crowd liked more than seeing a wingman find those extra gears and simply whoosh down the Popular Side touchline. So Albert's hasty return Down Under to join Cronulla Sharks in the NRL, after initially penning a new contract, left Saints with massive boots to fill.

Meli, however, had not come to St Helens to live in the shadow of his predecessor's memory with the robust 25-year-old vowing to make his own mark on the Knowsley Road flanks. A former New Zealand Warrior, with 14 Kiwi caps to his name at that point, he renewed his acquaintances with the boss who had coached him at club and Test level.

He said: "Daniel knows what to expect from me as a player and I know what to expect from him as a coach so we start straight away. We know how things are. I have found it really comfortable settling in here. The boys have made me really feel at home and everyone gets on.

"When I first signed I talked to guys like Vinnie Anderson, so I knew a little bit. I watched a few tapes of Saints games last year – particularly from the play-offs at the end of last season. They have plenty of flair and I know Daniel's style of coaching."

The contrast in playing styles between Albert and Meli was something fans would clearly soon pick up on. You only had to look at both men's physical make-up. Flyer Albert was a prolific try scorer at Saints, particularly in his final year when his telepathic link up with Jamie Lyon proved devastatingly productive. Although respectful of his predecessor's record, the strong-running Meli was keen to focus on his own game. And the powerful winger's record in NRL showed that he also knew his way over the whitewash.

"Darren Albert has done wonders at this club playing his best football at Saints. I have only had one club – New Zealand Warriors – and played my best football there. I play a different type of game. Although I have a lot of respect for Darren, he has gone and I am here to do a job and am looking forward to the start of the season," Meli said.

The powerful wing marked his debut in the friendly against Widnes by picking up the man of the match award after grabbing

25

a brace of tries and putting in a shuddering big tackle that echoed around the ground and dispossessed the Widnes ball carrier.

Meanwhile the imposing 6ft 5in, 17st frame of fellow Kiwi test player, front rower Cayless, had also cut a distinctive new figure on the Saints training ground. At 25, Cayless was at the peak of his powers for a prop and his size, good off-load game and ability to gallop for a big man were qualities that made him Anderson's first calling card signing.

The former Sydney Roosters prop, who joined on a four-year deal, had an unusual career-first to record – quite literally – at Ruskin Drive training ground in his first weeks at the club.

"I have swapped the sunshine and beach of Sydney for St Helens and I have trained in snow for the first time, which was so exciting that I had the camcorder out!" he said. This was 2006 – a little while before smart phones made such cumbersome kit obsolete.

After missing the 2005 Tri-Nations after needing an ankle operation, Cayless was looking forward to hitting the ground running after arriving in England three weeks earlier than anticipated. The last time home fans had seen the lanky front rower in the flesh was when he had a tangle with Saints skipper Paul Sculthorpe during Roosters' crushing win in the World Club Challenge match at a freezing cold Reebok in February 2003.

Cayless listed the challenge of playing attacking rugby and his wish to see Europe as influencing his decision to swap the prestigious Australian competition for the British Super League.

"Leaving the NRL – supposedly the premier competition – was a big decision to take. But I am looking forward to playing in Super League and will enjoy the free-flowing, attacking footy they play here. From the tapes I have seen of Saints they like to throw the ball about and attack as soon as they get an opportunity, even if it is in their own quarter.

"It is an exciting brand of footy they play and that is what thrills the crowds. You don't really see that in the NRL. Saints appear to be one of the best exponents of it. But coming from the Roosters where we had so much success, playing in three Grand Finals, I am looking forward to carrying that on at Saints. It is a strong squad –

practically the same as last year – with three more additions. There should be exciting times ahead," he said.

Cayless's link up with former Kiwi coach Daniel Anderson renewed an acquaintance that pre-dated their work together in the Test arena.

"Daniel used to referee school rugby in Sydney and he once sent me off for fighting. It was the first and only time I have been sent off as a player," Cayless said.

The new boys were welcomed to the club by skipper Paul Sculthorpe, who said: "Everyone who has seen them play knows what they can do. Leon Pryce had a great season with Bradford last year and played really well in a difficult Tri-Nations series. It was probably a big relief for him to settle his future by penning that deal with Saints and his performances have reflected that."

Although he arrived at the club slightly later, given he had been on Test duty with Great Britain, Leon Pryce, Saints' third big name recruit, lost no time to show his class with virtually every touch of the ball in the first team's only pre-season friendly at Widnes. Coach Daniel Anderson, who was not usually the biggest fan of pre-season warm up games, felt his new boys – and those around them – needed the run out game against Widnes if only to get used to each other.

He said: "We need to learn the new voices we have in our team; we have a different dynamic because we have three new players. The combinations with players around them and the way they complement others is hard to get on the training paddock without contact."

Pryce, whose sparkling form at the end of 2005 culminated in winning the Harry Sunderland award, was given the first chance to stake his claim on the stand off jersey.

Anderson said: "I don't see Leon having a problem in slotting in. He will complement our style of play – he is a very talented international player whose desire is to get close to the action. He will be given that first opportunity."

And, albeit just a warm-up game, the performance totally vindicated Anderson's view that the tall Bradfordian needed to be at the heart of the action at number six. Pryce's long passes yielded many of Saints' dozen tries in the 70-6 success – as they blasted off some cobwebs before heading off to Torremolinos for warm weather training.

Pryce – a teenage prodigy at the Bulls and one whose heart will always be with the Odsal club – soon felt at home. "It was a wrench to leave Bradford at first, but I have had four weeks here now and I feel really settled," he said.

"I was attracted to St Helens by the players that they have got here – good British players at that – and the style of rugby they play. On top of that having a few friends over here also helped."

Pryce joined Saints' Yorkshire Bus – the nickname given to the trans-Pennine travellers of himself, Nick Fozzard, Paul Anderson and Lee Gilmour – a quartet who crossed the Pennines every day for training.

Although the Saints coach had quickly declared his intentions with Pryce by handing the 24-year-old the number six shirt and offering him the chance to make that position his own, there was no advance discussion about positions ahead of the former Bull signing a three-year deal at Knowsley Road.

"I just wanted to come to a club that I thought could win trophies. At Bradford I always had respect for Saints, because they always had that knack of beating us in big games and finals.

"Now that I am a Saint myself I want to carry on that tradition," Pryce said.

Although the 6ft 1in, 16st 1lb international had played centre, full back and wing for both the Bulls and Great Britain, Saints had identified the previous season's Harry Sunderland winner as the man to give them real pace, power and penetration at stand off.

It was not just players who were settling in to the club. What turned out to be a vitally important piece of the backroom jigsaw was slotting into place, too – with technical adviser Alan Wilson taking up his post at Knowsley Road and Ruskin. The former New South Wales back rower took on a role to develop the talent at all levels of the club – not just the first teamers. And despite taking, what he described as his coldest training session ever with the under-17s shortly after his arrival, Wilson was another who had no regrets about swapping sunny Sydney for the bleak mid winter.

He said: "It is a tremendous hook over here to come to a proud club like St Helens with a world renowned reputation for rugby league. They want success here and that is what we want as coaches. But I don't just hang my hat on winning trophies – if you can improve players as individuals, you can take real pride in that."

As soon as he was appointed in November 2005, Wilson got to work whilst still in Sydney by trawling the internet.

"I read all the players' biographies and was immediately impressed by how many games these guys have played at the top level," he said.

He knew what to expect with the weather and claimed the people he met in St Helens during his opening two weeks had moaned about it more. However, the language difficulties, particularly from those with strong Yorkshire twangs, initially caused him some problems.

Wilson said: "In a few conversations I have just nodded because I have not understood a word they have said – especially Gilly. But the players have made my transition to St Helens really easy."

4

February

Saints were part of history when they kicked off their Super League campaign in the capital. The Londoners were going through one of their frequent re-invention phases, ditching the Broncos moniker, saying farewell to Brentford's Griffin Park and moving in lock, stock and jester's outfit with that most establishment of rugby union clubs – Harlequins. The Stoop ground is literally in the shadows of rugby union's Twickenham headquarters.

No doubt there were a few interested followers of the other code in the 8,213 crowd – as big a crowd as they would get down there – admittedly a figure swelled by more than 3,500 from St Helens. It is on days like that that you actually see how many fans Saints have in the capital. Plenty of those headed south to further their careers, others were no doubt forced down during the various recessions of the early 80s and early 90s – recessions that always bite harder into the lives and livelihoods of those up north.

The large turnout – including quite a few who had enjoyed the pre-match hospitality in the nearby Cabbage Patch or on the Fun Bus and Gerard Songsters journey down – made for a special atmosphere with plenty of singing. How many of those present that day really thought the season that was going to unfold would be so perfect?

The crowd witnessed some masterful passages of play, even if coach Daniel Anderson remarked afterwards that they had been interspersed with "ugly bits". There was plenty of stuff easy on the eye, though, with a debut try from Jason Cayless, a hat-trick from Paul Wellens, and further touchdowns from Ade Gardner and Jason Hooper helping Saints to a 40-16 victory.

But the pick of the scores both involved a piece of Jamie Lyon mastery. The first saw the Australian ace collect Sean Long's precision kick wide, before effortlessly slipping it to Gardner who did the rest. And then we saw another part of the Lyon armoury – a jack-hammer hand-off. When Lyon intercepted it looked a surefire score, but maybe a degree of ring-rustiness allowed him to be caught by Quins' covering prop Karl Temata. Undeterred, out came the Lyon palm and down went the lanky prop like a proverbial sack of spuds to allow the Aussie ace to wrap up the Saints scoring.

Assessing the game after video review Daniel Anderson said: "I was a little bit anxious ahead of our first game because we had not been able to have many friendlies beforehand. Although we were not great, we were ok and will get better as the year progresses.

"After the game we spoke about how there had been some great pieces of play as well as some ugly bits.

"There were quite a few positive features about the match. It was Sean Long's first game in five months since suffering that fractured cheekbone injury at Wigan. I thought Sean was great, but he will get better the more games he plays in addition to the more games he plays with Leon Pryce. Our half back combination is definitely going to be important to our chances this year.

"There were a lot of good performances on the day but Jason Cayless, Paul Wellens and Ade Gardner were the three players that really impressed upon analysis from the video.

"Saints version 2006 will continue to develop and although there are many players in the 2006 squad who have played together before, the team dynamic has changed with the addition of new players, myself and the new coaching staff in our first full off-season and the growing responsibility being placed by our ever improving young players."

Alas for those interested in spreading the game beyond the heartlands, the Quins experiment failed. They stuck around at the Stoop for eight seasons and despite it being Twickenham, a pleasant day out for northerners and the club providing a relaxed atmosphere, crowds dwindled year-on-year. Even the ditching of the Quins tag and reversion to Broncos could not arrest the decline – and they were to call it a day at the Stoop at the end of a poor 2013 and move out to Barnet.

More frustrating was that the professional club's struggle was in complete contrast to development at junior and amateur level. There have never been as many Londoners playing the sport – and making the grade too – but that has not been translated into turnstile clicks.

Back to the heartlands, for the second game the following Friday and more than 13,500 packed into an atmospheric Knowsley Road for first home game of the season – a match that saw a welcome return of skipper Paul Sculthorpe following a six month lay-off. Sculthorpe had undergone a major knee operation the previous August and started the game against newly promoted Castleford in the second row. Although the pugnacious Australian Hooper kept hold of the loose forward jersey, as a reward for a fine opening game, all eyes were on the two-time Man of Steel.

Ahead of the game coach Anderson explained: "Paul has done a huge amount of work, and physically he is very strong and refreshed. It is very hard when you get a very dynamic, dominant player in Super League like Paul, who is basically learning to ride a bike again. Last week he had a 'dusty day' at training which knocked his confidence a little bit, so I made the decision that he would not play. I have not seen anything this week to tell me he should not play.

"It is difficult for him because he cannot do what he has done for ten years. He simply does not have that dynamic movement. He will be able to do that in a couple of months. He is ready to go now, and is not going to get injured, his knee is not going to get any worse. It is simply a matter of him getting confidence."

Sculthorpe showed some good touches on his return in Saints' eight-try demolition of Super League new boys Castleford and had taken part in his own warming up ritual to minimise the chances of repeating the injury that had plagued him. He played almost three quarters of the game and tried to make the little things count, like the instinctive harrying and charge down of Cas scrum half Andy Kain's clearance kick that led directly to Jamie Lyon sending Long over for Saints' fourth try.

After the match Anderson said: "Scully has been such a high profile player and athlete for such a long time that he will obviously get media attention. He is so pleased to hear all the talk about him actually playing, because he was frustrated at being injured and explaining why he is not playing.

"In his career Scully has displayed many varied talents on the field, but his strongest asset is his strong running. His rehabilitation has allowed him to build himself up to be a formidable runner of the football and until he regains his touch after his long lay-off then we will see more of this."

2006 would turn out to be a tough, often frustrating year for Sculthorpe – a consummate professional, born leader and as tough a competitor as you would want on the field.

It was another one of Daniel's 'old, hard heads' on something of a comeback trail – Sean Long – that made a big difference. Playing only his second game since Terry Newton had made such an awful mess of his face on that fateful night at the JJB, the wily Wiganer earned the plaudits of his team-mates who picked him as their man of the match.

The match, alas, was something of an anti-climax after a blistering opening 40 minutes, which included a passage of play which saw the ball fly through eight pairs of hands before the Kiwi-Islander connection finished it off when centre Willie Talau sent Francis Meli over on his home debut.

The second half became an utterly tedious stop-start, error-ridden affair with the newly-promoted visitors seemingly being unable to cope with the pace of the game at the top level. The repeated shrill blasts of referee Ronnie Laughton's whistle plus a more dogged defensive display from the visitors in the second half combined to silence the large 13,528 crowd.

Despite chalking up two opening wins coach Daniel Anderson was understandably cautious, knowing full well that the big tests were to come from the Leeds, Bradfords and Hulls of this world. There was nevertheless a good degree of confidence that his troops would be ready for those bone-crunching conflicts to come.

He said: "We have had some tough moments in our first two matches but there has not been any sustained pressure applied against us. It may hit us at some stage in the game where we have to really batten down the hatches – something we have not had to do yet. But we are up to it."

Leeds Rhinos, who had suffered the ignominy of losing both major finals the previous season would be the first of the big beasts to bare their teeth. It was a challenge coach Anderson expected to be tough with the Saints boss seeing threats all over the park, not least at number six from a player that had tormented him in Great Britain colours when he was boss of the Kiwis – Danny McGuire. There was also a rare hint in Anderson's pre-match comments that defeat would not be disastrous and a degree of mitigation was put forward in advance.

"I have watched a bit of Leeds and both of us have gone into the season underdone because of the amount of players who played at the back end of last year and international commitments. We will be better after this game, no matter what happens. Leeds are a very classy team and very mentally resilient having been in every big game for the last two years," he said.

But Saints' version 2006 were not the sort of side to be trampled on, not least skipper Sculthorpe who demonstrated that when he dusted Leeds' perennial nuisance Ryan Bailey. When it came to 'Hey lads, hey' you wanted Sculthorpe in your corner – and it was no surprise to see him take to the boxing ring at the end of his playing career. The skipper's feistiness showed a team's unwillingness to be bullied – even if the disciplinary committee did take a dim view of that the following week.

It was a game that illustrated Saints' transformation from a side that had the view of 'you score 20 and we will score 30'. It is true, that attacking prowess had won them many admirers over the years and the nickname of the Entertainers, but it was their gutsy defensive display rather than flair with the ball that earned them a 13-4 win over the previous year's runners up.

Although it was by no means a classic – there were too many dropped balls for that – it was still an utterly enthralling encounter, which kept the 13,443 crowd on tenterhooks till the end. Interspersed between those errors, many of them forced by aggressive defence, there were some flashes of real brilliance with Leon Pryce's cut out pass to Francis Meli and Jamie Lyon's tackle on Danny Williams proving real game breakers.

The fact that Saints showed they did not have a soft underbelly and could lock horns with the toughest and come out on top was perhaps even more pleasing than the free scoring affairs they had treated their fans to on the previous two outings.

They were also lucky that the referee did not take further action against James Graham, whose clumsy late charge flattened half back Rob Burrow after the ball had gone. Graham was subsequently suspended for two matches and fined £350 for the challenge.

There was little separating the sides, but Saints' rock solid pack just about mastered Leeds' equally robust six with Paul Anderson and Sculthorpe producing an outstanding rolled-up sleeves effort. And at half back Pryce was head and shoulders above his opposite number McGuire to put down an early calling card for the GB stand off berth. For all the plaudits handed to Pryce, Lyon and Sculthorpe, arguably one of the most influential performances came from unsung hero James Roby, who pepped up Saints' attacking play with his incisive running.

The former Blackbrook Junior's fine break from deep inside Saints own half created the position for Lee Gilmour to plunge over to give Saints a half-time lead they would never relinquish. They had to battle for every metre, drop on every loose ball and eke out every point. And with the points on the board, they were able to keep Leeds at arm's length with that doggedness illustrated by the marvellous way Jason Hooper and Gilmour forced opposing full back Richie Mathers back over his line for a drop out.

So it was first blood to Saints in the battle of the big guns – with the weekend's other results leaving them with the only perfect record. Saints' third win in a row meant that the shaving foam was being liberally sprayed after the team had achieved their pre-season goal. The team had declared that they would not shave until they had chalked up three Super League victories, which led to some pretty iffy looking beards and some sad facial hair by the end of February.

Looking back, full back Paul Wellens explained: "It was something that Vinnie Anderson decided we should do. They had done it at New Zealand Warriors a few years previously when he was there.

"He said 'why don't we do it?' At that time I was not even sure that I could grow a full beard so was a bit reluctant. There were a few very dodgy facial hair growths at the end but those things in a small way galvanise the team."

5

Perelini and Wilson – the Backroom Boys

When Apollo Perelini landed in the world of rugby league in 1994 he came with a tough reputation and the nickname of The Terminator. It was fully justified, but if you come from the other code with a reputation like that, the hard men on the northern league circuit will test it out. With Perelini they soon stopped trying with Leeds' tough-nut wing John Bentley among those realising to his cost that the former Samoan rugby union World Cup flanker was the real deal. By the end of that first season Perelini was on his way to establishing himself one of the toughest, hardest running forwards in the 13-man code. Within two years he was winning silverware, helping Saints to bring home the Challenge Cup after a 20-year wait.

Perelini powered over for a try in that famous 'Ultimate Comeback' win at Wembley in 1996, and he grabbed a crucial four-pointer in the win at London that helped Saints edge Wigan out in the race to the inaugural Super League title. More success followed, with Perelini making an input into another Wembley success and two Grand Final wins before he returned to have three years back in rugby union with Sale.

He did not stay away long – in fact, with his home and roots remaining in the glass town, he never really left. But when he did come back to league and Saints in 2004 it was to have another big impact as a member of the backroom staff.

His job as strength and conditioning coach was an important one, and he really turned Saints' pack not simply into one of the biggest in the league but also one of the fittest. Although fitness was his brief, Perelini does not take personal credit for that, rather he points to the attitude and work ethic of the players who pushed themselves to the limit in the gym and got their rewards on the playing field.

Perelini explained: "The most important aspect of that year was that the club had a great culture of camaraderie and a great work ethic. We had guys who would turn up prior to training and do extras. It was such a great culture that nobody wanted to let anybody else down. If anybody had had a drink the night before they would turn up to training an hour early and do some extras

"The players that we had really cared for each other and really worked hard for each other and we had good coaching staff too."

One of Saints' big strengths in 2006 came in Perelini's own position in the front row. The club were well blessed with veteran Paul Anderson, Kiwi test prop Jason Cayless, the seasoned Nick Fozzard, rapidly advancing Samoan powerhouse Maurie Fa'asavalu and future England captain James Graham.

They were all different styles of prop, but Perelini's task was to deliver them to the coach in peak fitness. And he would be accountable to Daniel Anderson for that.

"We had some very good props that year and each knew their roles and responsibilities. My role was simply to up their strength and fitness – we did not just have some of the biggest props around, we also had some of the fittest.

"Paul Anderson did more minutes under me than he had ever done at Bradford and he loved it. He said 'just pull me off when I am ready' – and I was always looking to see if he was ready. However both myself and Daniel would always get it in the neck from Paul if we dragged him off too early – he just loved being on the field. All of our front rowers – James Graham, Jason Cayless, Nick Fozzard and Maurie Fa'asavalu, wanted to be on the field."

Fa'asavalu had followed an almost identical path to league as Perelini – the powerhouse islander also coming from an impressive rugby union World Cup with Samoa to wearing the red vee. Admittedly, it took Fa'asavalu a little longer to really bed in, but he was another player who came on leaps and bounds under Daniel Anderson – although the Saints boss credits the input of the old heads around him.

The winter of 2005/06 saw Perelini take charge of Daniel Anderson's first pre-season training. It is one that saw them go into the winter fuelled by plenty of motivation after the way 2005 had ended.

"We had such belief in ourselves, and the players we had believed in themselves. We had missed out in the Challenge Cup the year before and we had dipped out in the play-offs due to the injuries, all we could think of was those cups that we missed out on.

"Ahead of 2006 our pre-season was perfect we worked very hard. We went away to Spain where we did a lot of hard, honest toil – the boys worked very hard but came back ready and raring to go. We started the season on fire," Perelini said.

Assisted by the new equipment supplied by Powerzone, the team found their shape – quite literally. Some tough sessions on the mats of the St Helens Judo Hall were supervised by Roy Wood and Gerry Birchall, delivering some new defensive techniques that helped tick another box on the Daniel Anderson coaching blueprint.

The Saints coach said: "The players went through some pain in the training during the winter but it built a great base for the tough season ahead."

Anderson knew exactly where he wanted his players to be – and it was Perelini's job to deliver a set of players that had dynamism, power and endurance.

Perelini explained: "When I went into coaching I became responsible for every detail of how these players turn out. So on a match day if I have a front rower that can't last 15 minutes then that is my responsibility. I knew that.

"But it also gave me a lot of joy to see guys improve and push themselves to the limit. The satisfaction is a lot different as a coach than it was for me as a player. You can walk away and say 'job well done'. It is particularly pleasing when all the hard work of planning strategies comes to fruition – especially when your team wins titles and Challenge Cups."

In 2006 success in the Challenge Cup was the first target, if only because that was physically the first piece of silverware that they could get their hands on. Perelini had won that trophy twice as a player and had been on the staff when Saints took it out again in May 2004 – the last big thing the club had won if you discount the League Leaders' Shield.

With the final in August it was no longer an early part of the season campaign, it ran throughout the course of the year. Perelini explained how the staff and team tackled it.

"With something like the Challenge Cup campaign we worked backwards rather than forwards, starting with the final, knowing each game what we would be doing and making sure that we would not be peaking too early and ensuring that we would be coming good at the right stage. When these things fall into place it gives a great deal of satisfaction," he said.

The Saints team of 2006 was something of a who's who of rugby league featuring some absolute legends of the British game complemented by a good smattering of top overseas stars who were in the prime of their playing careers. The antipodeans of '06 were not here to wind down at a slower pace or simply enhance their pension pots. These were players who still wanted to push the boundaries and there were undoubtedly egos that went with that. But for all those big characters, shrewd observer Perelini noticed that there were not any cliques in the Knowsley Road dressing rooms.

"It was an unbelievable season. We had some talent and some great guys. It was such a close knit group but I can't think of any cliques – and I would be the first person to spot them. There were none. Everyone in that team was in it together and close-knit and tight.

"We all trained, drank and ate together – we were very close so when it came to the on field performance and the guys were prepared to put their bodies on the line for their mates," Perelini declared.

The likeable Samoan was recently inducted into the Saints Hall of Fame, something he accepted proudly on a whistle stop trip back from Dubai, where he now works. That honour was bestowed largely in recognition of his time as a player, but his off the field work was invaluable and worthy of recognition too.

Technical adviser Alan Wilson was another member of the backroom staff who added value to each member of the squad that year. He may not have been that visible to the fans – but several years after his departure the players that had worked with him were very keen to pay tribute to his hands-on approach in improving a full range of skills, from passing, catching and kicking through to the wrestling techniques that were now invaluable to executing the tackle.

Although he had played Origin for New South Wales and had even had a stint in Super League with Bradford Bulls, Wilson was anything but a household name in British rugby league. But he had been there and done it and had already worked with Daniel Anderson at Parramatta. He was fully in tune with his job description that initially caused a bit of head scratching among supporters because for one reason or another he was not classed as an assistant coach.

On taking on the post Wilson said: "My job is to assist Daniel in any way he wants but I can help the players in the smaller parts of their game. Things like the way they pass, catch and kick. We have already started to work on those things and it is about having an eye for those details. The players have been very receptive already."

Those players lapped it up with a then still developing Jon Wilkin in particular grateful for advice on things to improve his game.

Wilkin explained: "Alan Wilson's input was priceless that year. He got us together on a 'Tuesday extras club' – so we'd go out for a beer on a Monday and then he'd get us together on a Tuesday to do a bit of fitness and a bit of skill.

"On our day off we would have 12-15 players doing extras. He'd try to get me kicking and I'm 100 per cent certain his input made James Graham into the ball-playing front rower he is today. He helped me kick and pass better, and did likewise with the wrestling. At that time I was probably one of the best wrestlers in the competition and that was down to Alan. I owe him."

Wilson's technical expertise and ability to pass that on and the culture that created, was also picked up on by Paul Wellens.

He said: "Alan Wilson was excellent. What he did was spend a lot of time working with people on individual skills. On days off he'd say 'I'm in, come in!' And that created a really professional culture. A lot of young players would say to themselves, 'I am not having a day off'.

"It was not a case of over exerting yourself, but it was a case of spending 40 minutes working on individual skills. It became habit – for the first week it was two or three and then it ended with 15 to 19 players going in on their day off. Alan was a big driver in that. He was also good with the video sessions in picking up technical aspects we could improve on, and with the good players that we had they were able to go out and improve that the week after."

6

March

March – as my mam was often fond of saying – always comes in like a lion and goes out like a lamb. In 2006 it was less a lion, more of a snow leopard and there was a generous smattering of the white stuff scattered across a bitterly cold Halliwell Jones Stadium for Saints' derby clash with the Wire.

It was a clash that was slowly but surely developing some history – especially at the HJ. This was, of course, the scene of the previous year's Lazarus-style comeback when Saints looked down and out when Graham Appo's converted try left them trailing 16-4 and the Wolves drummer was in overdrive with just eight minutes left on the clock.

Unbelievably, tries from Darren Albert, Mickey Higham and, with the last play of the match, acting captain Keiron Cunningham sparked jubilation in the away end, prompting an excitable coach Ian Millward to run on to the pitch afterwards. Basil was still pumped with the effects of the tumultuous events when he was asked to give his press conference in the stand. He declined, opting to do it on the playing field and his exchange with Wolves press officer Gina Coldrick contributed to his departure a few weeks later.

So, it was a fixture that had meaning, particularly for success-starved Wolves who were real big club wannabes after spending so long in Saints' shadow, having won just one of the clashes between the sides in the summer era.

So when Saints headed to Warrington without skipper Sculthorpe and James Graham, who had both been banned by the judiciary, and missing prop Nick Fozzard with medial knee ligament damage, the Wolves may have been licking their lips.

Optimism – however misplaced – was never in short supply in Warrington – a feeling picked up by Saints' fans who now taunt them with the words 'It's always your year!'

It was going to be a toughie with just one recognised prop on the bench – impact player Maurie Fa'asavalu, but it was one in which we saw Keiron Cunningham bring his physicality to the table to compensate for the absent big-hitters. Saints had a real warrior leader in Cunningham. Although it never tends to be the forwards that catch the eye of man of the match awarders looking too much at the 'tries and breaks' men, Cunningham's weighty contribution counted for much. And that was probably only really noticed when he was on the bench for a breather, a period that coincided with a Wolves rally.

Coach Anderson was not among those missing the significant contribution of the powerhouse Saints number nine, declaring: "I thought Keiron Cunningham was really outstanding out there. For the first time this season he picked the ball up and really got over the advantage line and proved to be a real handful. Keiron was hard to stop and got us on a roll whenever he carried the ball. Defensively he also just whacked anybody who came near him. He is really getting match fit now. Although I thought he was wonderful last year, I am excited about what he can bring to the team this year."

Initial worries about the team being weakened were quickly dispelled and for a few moments in the first half it looked like it was going to be one of those old fashioned Wolves games of an earlier Super League era – the ones were Saints could comfortably declare at half-time.

Leading 12-0, Saints had withstood everything the Wolves had thrown at them and big Paul Anderson crashed on to Sean Long's pass to touch down, nearly taking the referee over with him – this one harshly chalked off for a forward pass.

It was a far from pretty encounter – turning into something of a kicking duel with Long and Lee Briers testing out the cold fingers of both full backs with steepling up and unders. Not that ex-Saints stand off Briers had an easy ride, with the dogged Jason Hooper rattling him after he had launched his first kick in the second minute and repeating the dose – sending him sprawling to the floor – later on in the game to get ten minutes in the sin-bin

Anderson was delighted with the gutsy, gritty win which showed that although they favoured the dry grounds, they were a team for all seasons. He said: "You have to play to both the conditions and the opposition. It was not an evening for flamboyant football, the conditions ensured that it was an arm wrestle and a tough game. Once again our display showed that we are going to compete in every facet of the game – pressurising the opposing kickers, tackling and kicking.

"The wintry conditions were a new experience for me and I popped out on the afternoon of the game and the snowflakes were as big as dinner plates, so I was amazed that the game went ahead. There was nothing wrong with the surface – it just looked different with the covering of snow."

Once again Saints' new found steel in defence was clearly illustrated with a potent attacking team limited to two tries, one of them coming when they were down a man. It was not all about the structures and systems Anderson had put in place, the Saints boss put a big emphasis on the attitude of that – on this occasion – thin blue line.

Anderson said: "We are very motivated at the moment and there are a number of factors behind our defensive prowess. The players are very proud – we do a lot of training on defence and try to educate the players on how to make good decisions.

"But ultimately you are not going to be a good defensive team if you don't have courage or don't want to tackle. In those circumstances it does not matter what defensive system you use you are going to miss them."

The ground was still cold the following week when Saints crossed the Pennines to Huddersfield without Sean Long, who was out with an eye injury, and suffered further disruption when interchange hooker James Roby was pulled out sick. Both absentees were missed and as hard as youngsters Scott Moore and Matty Smith tried at scrum half, Saints missed Long's dominance and ability to push the side around the pitch.

It was not the prettiest of games, but Saints survived a late scare in perishing conditions to preserve their perfect record with another hard fought 18-16 victory in the land of the Giants.

Although Saints got off to a dream start when Ade Gardner waltzed around his younger brother Mat for a try after 45 seconds, they had to battle for another 79 minutes to take the spoils with Huddersfield's two leviathans Wayne McDonald and Eorl Crabtree proving a handful in the middle for a pack missing Nick Fozzard and James Graham.

Saints finally got on top in that score with Maurie Fa'asavalu, complemented by a particularly aggressive tackling stint from Keiron Cunningham, standing up to be counted. The sheer physicality of the brutal, bruising but often dour, tussle in the middle made it even more illuminating when we saw a flash of Jamie Lyon magic. The Australian ace magnificently cut inside to dash in at pace after the long-striding Leon Pryce had pierced the line and ate up 60 metres in the build up. It showed the value of Lyon – a player who would always be able to come up with something special when the going was tough.

Saints were back on home turf – at a newly smoke-free Knowsley Road – when they faced the only other unbeaten team in Super League – Bradford Bulls. And a monumental war of attrition was predicted by Saints boss Daniel Anderson, who described the reigning champions the Bulls as having "monsters everywhere".

Anderson said: "I am sure Bradford will be a very tough game. They are going well, but the conditions are conducive to fairly tight play. They also have two very good experienced half backs and monsters everywhere. They have no problems going forward, and with the conditions being as they are there are a lot of bash ups and battles which they relish."

Saints fielded three former Bulls – Paul Anderson, Lee Gilmour and Leon Pryce – with the latter facing his former club for the first time.

"Players like to play against their old clubs. I am sure Leon will high-five a few of his former colleagues as they come in. Then he will do his best to terrorise them when he is out on the park. I am sure he will be up for it. I am happy with the way Leon is progressing – he is taking more steps forward than backward,"

Anderson said.

The undercurrent of unfinished business must have been to the fore when it came to tackling certain teams in 2006. And Bradford, of course, were the team that ended injury-depleted Saints' hopes of making it to the Grand Final the previous term, edging an utterly absorbing play-off game at Knowsley Road.

"Bradford were on form then, and although we played well, they played better. The aim on Friday night is to win. If they are to beat us again they are going to have to play very, very well," Anderson said.

And so they did. Saints made it six wins out of six, with their 38-16 success sending Bradford to their first defeat since the previous July. In fact, Saints would have won it at a canter had the otherwise impressive Sean Long not bombed a glorious scoring chance seven minutes after the break. With no Bulls men in sight, Long dived prematurely and the ball came loose on impact and bobbled away. When the video ref rightly ruled no try, Long looked around desperately hoping for a hole to appear and swallow him.

The 'diving' error was the only blemish on Long's night's work which saw him poach one try, set up at least two others and routinely punish the Bulls with some magnificent kicking including a 40-20.

Saints coach Daniel Anderson said he did not have to say anything to Long about his howler, but added: "He copped an absolute hiding in the dressing room. He is just hoping he was not making any stupid faces before he lost the ball. Longy was wonderful. He is a different style of player in the last 12 months and has been a little bit more direct."

The early signs were ominous for Saints with the Bulls on the scoresheet first when Paul Deacon's high kick to the corner went through the hands of wing Francis Meli allowing Ben Harris to zip in for the touchdown. Although the Bulls dominated the opening quarter they failed to penetrate what was once again a magnificent Saints defence.

It was turning into a bruising encounter with Saints losing full back Paul Wellens on 23 minutes with a suspected broken cheekbone when bravely diving on a loose ball. Saints simply slotted Pryce to full back, where he remained defensively sound and linked up well in attack, and drafted Jon Wilkin in off the bench. Wilkin relished the opportunity to be in the thick of the action and had possibly his best game in Saints colours.

It became Saints' best attacking display of the season with the under-rated Willie Talau taking the flick pass out of the Jamie Lyon repertoire to send Meli in, being followed over the whitewash by Long and Pryce – his first in the red vee – in a 15 minute spell.

But Saints temporarily lost loose forward Jason Hooper, who was sin-binned for the second time in three games following a late tackle on Deacon, and the visitors made their numbers tell with Shontayne Hape's converted try cutting the deficit to four points at the break. But to illustrate what key component Long's kicking was to this side – he kept his composure on the sixth tackle to loft a high kick to Ade Gardner, who first tapped it back and then cashed in on the bounce to dot it down.

Then he launched a brilliant 40/20 to lay the perfect platform for Saints to finish it off with tries from Keiron Cunningham, a 90 metre charge upfield from Meli and Gardner's second – this courtesy of the Lyon flick.

Saints had, for the first time that season, produced a fine attacking performance to complement their stubborn defence. Something Anderson picked up on in his press conference immediately after the match.

"It was a bust-out game for us. The conditions this season have meant that we have played conservatively. They let their chains loose on their own ability tonight. We'll take confidence out of the game, attacking wise. We needed to learn to attack and back ourselves and we did a few things tonight that we haven't done before," he said.

Having had a few days to reflect and review the game Anderson praised the contribution of the 17-man collective but singled out the individual performances of Keiron Cunningham and Sean Long as "outstanding".

Anderson said: "Keiron's form in the past month has been awesome. He is a real professional and, although as coaches we have been giving him minor adjustments to try and make him an even better player, the credit goes to Keiron for taking the bit between his teeth with his game. As a hooker, if he decides to do something on the pitch it will get done – better than anyone else in the world.

"Longy, meanwhile, has taken plenty of stick for diving short of the try-line and spilling the ball. Because of the scoreline we can laugh about it. And it's also water off a duck's back to him, which was demonstrated by his crucial 40/20 kick."

Another concern for the Saints boss was Hooper's second sin-binning in three weeks for his challenge on the opposition kickers. He said: "I've spoken to Stuart Cummings to discuss the interpretation of the rules regarding pressurising the kickers and dangerous throws. I have acknowledged that these players are performing roles that I have instructed them to for the team. We will modify our pressuring of the kicker and the RFL will ensure that our players are not placed in unsafe, compromising tackles which involve a dangerous throw."

Hull's KC Stadium had been the scene of some real horror days and nights for Saints since it first opened in 2003, with a record of four defeats. But sitting pretty at the top of the pile coach Daniel Anderson played down the significance of the stadium being a bogey ground for his side, choosing to concentrate on the form that saw Saints produce their finest attacking display of the season against Bradford.

He said: "I am sure Hull will be up for us – but we are playing a confident brand of rugby at the moment and if Hull want to beat us they are going to have to be good."

He was right – Saints were white-hot in rattling in 46 points without reply to bury that hoodoo and see off poor John Kear from his job seven months after guiding the Black and Whites to a Challenge Cup victory.

Key to victory was a tremendous first quarter display from front rowers Jason Cayless, Paul Anderson and Keiron Cunningham. They then received good back up off the bench from the explosive Maurie Fa'asavalu and the solid-as-a-rock James Graham. Given that this was the area where the Hull props like Jamie Thackray and Garreth Carvell had the ascendancy in last year's miserable

Challenge Cup semi-final, the triumph was doubly symbolic for Saints.

As the nil part of the scoreline suggests, this game was not just about silky Saints scoring skills, but the grunt and fire that saw three defenders consistently rock the Airlie Birds back on their heels. With that aspect of their game sorted, Saints attack clicked into gear as they gained in confidence and relished the room earned by the pack's effort.

Leon Pryce's second try on the hour mark summed up the self belief and willingness to keep the ball alive – with the ball going left, right and centre through nine pairs of hands before the Saints stand off brushed past Hull full back Shaun Briscoe to touch down. But for one perplexing decision from the video ref who somehow spotted a knock-on in the build up to a Lyon 'try' Saints would have racked up a half century.

So another bogey was laid to rest, and a crescendo of boos rang around the KC from disgruntled home fans, with Saints' jubilant 1,100 travelling army taunting 'Are you Wigan in disguise?' The basis of that chant lay in the sight of Saints' old foe from the other side of the lump languishing at the bottom of the Super League pile.

Attention at the end of the month switched to the Challenge Cup and Anderson took no chances ahead of the team's opening tie against Doncaster with a strong side selected with a couple of minor adjustments. Anderson explained: "There is no difference to the way we approach this game than we would a match with Bradford or Hull, we are just getting about our business. Our aim is to win the game and so the team I'll put out will be a very serious one.

"There won't be wholesale changes or a group of young St Helens boys getting their first start in the senior team. Doncaster will approach this game with plenty of enthusiasm and will enjoy the prospect of playing against some superstars, even though it may be a bit daunting for them."

As it turned out it was neither the prettiest nor most memorable of matches with Saints winning 56-6, with the minnows grabbing a consolation try in the last minute to spoil the clean sheet.

There were a few jitters at first with the game being scoreless at 19 minutes until Keiron Cunningham's route-one rumble over the line. From there on in Saints scored almost at will getting the job done without playing anywhere near their best.

In a way the ineffectiveness of the Doncaster tackling forced Saints off script, leading to some uncharacteristic errors. Anderson put his finger on it: "In Super League the defences are extremely effective with usually two or three men in there. In the game versus Doncaster there were occasions when the tackles were not that effective, so players were looking to promote the ball.

"The style of game they were trying to play was quite different to what we would normally play. Instead of trying to build pressure and allow opportunities to present themselves, we were trying to score off every play, which provided our undoing."

7

Jamie Lyon – the Second Wizard of Aus

Where do you start with Jamie Lyon? The sublimely skilful centre had plenty to live up to when he first signed on the dotted line with the billing as the club's biggest capture since Mal Meninga. After all Big Mal's name was etched indelibly into the town's sporting folklore after leading the club out of a seven-year trophy drought in 1984/85. But two eventful seasons in the red vee saw the Aussie ace surpass those expectations with a string of consistently stunning displays which earned him a cult status on the terraces.

His quick feet, sublime handling skills and remarkable strike rate of 46 tries and 213 goals in 63 appearances established Lyon as a player that will still be talked about 20 years down the line.

Sometimes it is hard to believe that the Australian superstar, seven years later still ranked up there among the world's top ten players, actually swapped Sydney for St Helens for those two wonderful years. It is even harder to take in nowadays, given the strength of the Australian dollar in relation to sterling compared to the exchange rate of the noughties. And then factor in the cash that has gone in to boost the appeal and prestige of NRL that means the elite players have no reason whatsoever to leave Australia.

It is a strange trait, prevalent but not exclusive to St Helens, but all the time Lyon was terrorising the opposition, flicking out sublime passes, scoring impossible tries and kicking goals for fun, too many folk spent time and energy pessimistically speculating. Would he arrive, if he'd get home sick and leave, whether he would return for a second stint – and then – as two glorious years drew to a glittering close – when he would be coming back? Half way through his first season – at the time of the Millward saga – his name got dragged into the debate between those backing the chairman and supporters of the newly fired boss. If you took Millward's side Lyon was signed by the ex-coach and his dad Bob, if you were a club loyalist the deal was hammered out by Eamonn McManus. And of course, at the press conference announcing Millward signing a three-and-a-half year contract at the JJB there was this mischievous hint that Lyon would be joining his former boss at Wigan.

For all that debate, maybe Saints fans can with absolutely certainty thank Millward for Lyon's arrival. For, if the Saints boss hadn't sent a weakened team to Bradford on that fateful Easter Monday, 2004, centre Martin Gleeson would never have had the opportunity to slip down to a Wigan bookmaker. The nimble-footed, slick-handling Gleeson, then at his peak and in the Great Britain set-up, would never have been banned; he would not have subsequently been sold to Warrington and therefore Saints would not have been sniffing for a centre. It's an ill wind and all that.

But for those who enjoyed the silky-skilled action rather than having anxiety attacks about any sub-plots, Lyon's performances in the red vee were just a joy to behold. Lyon, with his ability to stand up his marker or markers and create space for his wingman was pure magic.

Lyon arrived at Saints – via a stint at country club Wee Waa Panthers – after walking out on Parramatta and NRL citing disenchantment with big game football and saying he was sick of Sydney. Given his contract with the Eels only expired at the end of 2006, no other NRL club would have been allowed to tap him up. It fell into place perfectly for Saints, with the Australian press quoting figures of $150,000 to clear Lyon's existing contract at the Eels as well as $600,000 salary split over two seasons.

No sooner had the ink dried on the contract, the Saints chairman Eamonn McManus was forced to go on the defensive in the Australian press telling the *Sun-Herald*: "Jamie has obviously been a bit unsettled over there, but when I talked to him I found him to be a very level-headed young fellow who is very excited about coming over here.

"He is keen to do something different and he sees this as a great opportunity. We don't see it as a risk.

"We dealt with Jamie, with his uncle, Mick Smith, who looked after the deal for him from over there, and Parramatta officials Denis Fitzgerald and Greg Mitchell and it was a straightforward deal. It was all done in a dignified manner and now we're looking forward to what Jamie can bring to the club.

"I don't think there's any more chance of Jamie wanting to up and leave St Helens early than there would be with any other player. He was looking for a clean start."

Lyon had a wow of a season in 2005, striking up a great rapport with blond speedster Darren Albert and waltzing off with the Man of Steel and Player of the Year awards as well as scoring 24 tries. But with Albert returning Down Under, Lyon would have a new partner to offer gifts to during the course of 2006 and Ade Gardner blossomed as a result.

However, even before a ball had been kicked in anger in 2006 the speculation Down Under was fairly frenzied as to where Lyon would be playing his rugby the following season. However, the Wizard of Aus's primary focus was having another top year in the red vee. Lyon said: "First thing is first – I want to have a good season and work the other things out at a later date. Staying in St Helens after this year is something worth thinking about. It has been a positive for me playing here and it has helped my game. When things are going your way and you enjoy your rugby, you become comfortable.

"I am hoping for some trophies and to play some good footy in the process. We were not that far away last year, we had a couple of injuries but I don't want to make excuses. We have a bigger and better squad this year. Saints have bought really well, they have added a bit of size and a lot of skill. Overall we have pieced together a great squad."

And that year went to plan, with the bloke outside him cashing in, with Ade Gardner becoming Saints' leading scorer with 31 tries. Lyon's rapport with the then 22-year-old Barrovian was productive and was built both on and off the field, starting the previous season, car sharing to training from Rainford – the northern semi-rural suburb of St Helens borough.

Gardner said: "Me and Jamie were good mates because he had moved into Rainford the previous year and only lived up the road from me, so we would get in the car to training together and go out for a beer on a weekend."

But it was on the field that the link-up provided sparks and more importantly points – and with points came prizes. Gardner did explain that he needed a sixth sense and eyes in the back of his head at times to collect the money ball that would find itself being propelled out of the Lyon palm despite the attention of one, two and even three defenders.

"It became abundantly clear just training with Jamie that I had to expect anything. The ball could come at any time and in pre-season training I tried to get that in my head and sure enough, when the season started, that was the case. Some of Jamie's offloads were unbelievable – but I knew the passes were coming. It got to a stage in that 2006 season when we would get in situations and parts on the field where I thought 'we are going to score here'. I would know what to expect. And sure enough we did," Gardner said.

Everyone knows about the silky skills of the man, the pace and his uncanny knack of giving his opponent the slip. However, Gardner believes his former right hand man does not get the plaudits he deserves for his pure dogged will to win. Lyon also had a way of geeing up those around them and making sure they were always on their mettle.

"He was such a joy to play alongside and such a competitor as well. I don't think he gets enough credit for that part of his make-up. He was a proper winner who would not give up on anything, any kick chase, a break by our team or chasing the opposition down.

"For such an easy going bloke and one who was quite a shy, laid-back lad he would have a pop at you if you were not on your game. He was a real, proper winner.

"His attitude rubbed off on me a bit. I recall Sean Long's try at Twickenham in the Challenge Cup Final where Jamie slipped it to me and I instinctively offloaded back inside to Longy, who did the rest. Playing alongside him gave you an almost contagious confidence.

"When Jamie signed and Eamonn came in and told us we could not believe it. He was a bit of an enigma who had played Origin for New South Wales, Test matches for Australia and in the NRL Grand Final. We were not sure how it was going to go down here in St Helens, but what a cracking player. It took him a while to get going but once he clicked it was frightening – he could do absolutely anything on the park. He is a quiet, shy lad but if he came back tomorrow we would be best mates again in five minutes," Gardner said.

Lyon had another wow of a season in 2006 with a try in the opener against Harlequins being the prelude to another 21 that year, scoring 164 goals through the uprights to put the top hat on it. His star quality shone through, even in a crackerjack team of all talents.

Full back Paul Wellens saw at first hand how Lyon grew into that team, taking off as the grounds dried out to allow him to display his full repertoire of talents. Wellens said: "When you talk about players having an impact, Jamie Lyon is up there with Mal Meninga in terms of the impact he had on the club at the time. I remember going to pick him up from the airport with Paul Sculthorpe in 2005. We knew he had walked out on Parramatta and could get a bit homesick so we thought we had better get him settled in quickly, thinking it best for us to pick him up rather than someone from the club who he did not really know and was not familiar with.

"We picked him up and he looked overweight with shabby hair and me and Scully looked at each other and kind of thought 'what the bloody hell is this?' He looked like a caveman walking through the airport. But he was a cracking fella, and quite quiet too.

"I remember his first five or six games for Saints in the February and early March of 2005. It was boggy and wet and therefore we never got to see him in full flow. But as soon as the grounds dried up Jamie went into overdrive. I had never seen anything like it."

Although Saints had a team of stars and a monster pack and

were usually on the right side of the scoreboard, there were times when Lyon could pull something out of the fire to get the team home. The close game against Salford at the old Willows ground was a classic example, with Lyon conjuring up three tries. Wellens recalls another game in the summer of the previous season when Saints had rested a few and struggled to raise their game at relegation-battling Leigh at a by then dilapidated Hilton Park.

He said: "I was not playing, and Keiron was on the bench with Jamie. We were a bit busted and we were struggling a bit but then Daniel threw Jamie on and it was try, kick off and try – job done. It was kind of 'thanks for coming, Jamie'." Lyon's two tries were the difference that day in preventing a shock defeat.

In 2006 Lyon got better from week one at Harlequins and although the dry tracks of summer helped, there was also a sharpening of his focus for the business end evidenced by his hat-trick in the penultimate league game of the campaign. Winning the Grand Final and winner's ring that went with it was all Lyon was thinking about, particularly after already tasting defeat in a Grand Final Down Under with Parramatta in 2001.

The emotion of it being his final game in the red vee, was not something that was playing on his mind. Speaking ahead of the game at the pre-match press conference at Old Trafford Lyon said: "You play all year to get into the Grand Final. We are playing pretty well at the moment, but so are Hull so it should be a cracking game.

"I don't think too much about it being my last game – it will probably hit me more after the match. I'm just carrying on training hard and looking forward to it.

"I will miss St Helens and it has been really good to me. The club has been great and the fans have been absolutely awesome and my team-mates especially have made me feel welcome from the day I first arrived," Lyon said.

"There were a lot of doubters at the start, but I did not think about it too much because what they were all talking about was never in my mind. Everyone here has been great and so it is going to be sad to go."

His six points in the final were the last contributions to a

610-point haul

Statistics alone though could not do the story of Lyon's time at Saints justice. In a modern professional game where much emphasis is placed on raw power, bulk and pace, Jamie displayed a subtlety and skill that rekindled British rugby league fans' appreciation of the finer points of centre play.

Team-mates will vouch that Lyon is the most skilful player they have played with – praise indeed, bearing in mind the calibre of stars that have graced Knowsley Road in the Super League era – while supporters have marvelled at his magical handling skills, twinkled-toed running and brilliant cover tackling.

"It was just phenomenal what he could do – he was really skilful and super quick. I don't think people realised just how quick he was, but if he got away nobody caught him," Wellens said.

8

April

Saints had some high profile visitors from rugby union in April with Saracens coaches Mike Ford and ex-Wallaby boss Alan Jones being guests of Daniel Anderson, who declared: "They spent the day with us and we bounced off each other. For my professional development and that of the coaching staff I feel it is imperative that we get to other codes."

Anderson was always thinking about the next step, and open to new ideas. However, in April it was the playing and training pitches that were at the forefront of his mind after a soggy opening two months of the season. The conditions had not allowed 'the Entertainers' to really cut loose as much as they would have liked with the personnel they had on board. It was not just the match day conditions under foot that Anderson had a concern about, but for a long spell the team were struggling for a quality practice pitch.

Anderson said: "Conditions are very difficult at the moment because the Knowsley Road pitch is currently soft and shifting. To use the racehorse terminology we have a number of players who are 'top of the ground' players who are playing well in boggy conditions, but will relish playing on the firmer pitches. Saints, along with a lot of other teams, will get better once the pitches dry out.

"The soggy conditions are causing problems and our biggest issue at the moment is field training availability. Unfortunately we have been unable to access any quality pitches over the last month. The same predicament applies to the Academy teams.

"There is only one way to develop promising local talent into possible Super League players and that is gym training combined with suitable diet and field sessions. The lack of field sessions means that players with natural ability are developing slowly and it is a frustration for the coaches and players alike as they want to improve."

Anderson was talking ahead of a challenging three games in 11 days programme that commenced with a 16-6 win over Harlequins played in diabolical conditions. The weather was so freakishly bad that Quins skipper Mark McLinden was forced to change his sodden jersey halfway through the second half because he had concerns about hypothermia.

The weather made it a real war of attrition but the game was marked by Paul Wellens' 100th career try after winning the race to collect Sean Long's delicate chip over the visiting full back to charge over.

It was a vital try, putting Saints into a slender 10-6 lead – and was the only difference between the sides until substitute prop James Graham drove over 10 minutes from the end. The unseasonal weather and Wellens' landmark score may have grabbed the headlines, but it was the Great Britain full back's work in defence that was the key to Saints' victory.

With the driving rain and swirling wind causing massive problems, Harlequins' half back Luke Dorn took advantage of the conditions to pepper Saints' line with a succession of high bombs and tricky grubbers. But Wellens was equal to the task defusing each kick with aplomb and driving the ball away from his line.

Anderson said: "The conditions were atrocious but the players dug in and ground out the result. I don't think I have ever seen a set of blokes come in for a shower as quickly as my boys did after the game.

"The weather was as bad as I have seen a match played in because the rain was bitterly cold and virtually horizontal. It was quite bizarre because both teams struggled for motivation – hardly any of the players wanted to be out there at the back end because they had been drenched by ice cube cold water for the duration of the game. In Friday's tough conditions I thought our back three of Ade, Wello and Francis were fantastic and played with a lot of maturity."

From there league-leading Saints tackled a Wigan side still rooted to the foot of the table and facing relegation for the first time since infamously dropping into Division Two in 1980. It was thought Wigan's shock sacking of coach Ian Millward days before the game would add an unknown ingredient to what is traditionally the most intense and tempestuous fixtures in the Super League calendar.

The axing of the former Saints boss – his second high profile dismissal in less than a year – came after a string of poor results in charge at Wigan, which had left them anchored to the foot of the table. It prompted plenty of terrace humour with plenty of Saints fans dubbing Basil 'Agent Millward'. Wigan's woes were in stark contrast to the way unbeaten Saints had started the season turning the Good Friday clash into a first against last encounter for the first time in living memory.

Skipper Paul Sculthorpe – a veteran of many a derby clash – said: "You don't expect a Saints v Wigan game to be a top v bottom, but it is a massive game nonetheless. It always is and I am sure that they will raise their game.

"The atmosphere brings it out and we are expecting a tough game. But we will just look to make sure our own house is in order and if we play like we can the result will follow."

Coach Anderson had been fed all the tales of how supposed weakened Wigan teams had beaten so-called stronger Saints line-ups in the past, but concentrated on preparing his team.

"I am not fazed by playing Wigan because we have a good squad full of confidence, with a lot of motivation, hunger, plenty of enthusiasm and competition for places. I am very confident that we will win the game as long as we prepare well. If we don't show Wigan the respect they deserve then we will make it hard for ourselves. Every Wigan player will have to play at the top of their game to beat us.

"I won't need to talk to the players about the importance of this game – I have enough players here who are St Helens born and bred or have played a number of Saints v Wigan derbies and know the emotion that goes with this game.

"I am under no illusions about how tough it will be. I will also be warned by some of my players, who may talk about how supposedly weak Wigan teams have won Good Friday games in the past. All I will say on that score is that did happen in the past – we are a much more mature, professional outfit and at the moment we are coping well with expectations. Our results are a reward for the way we are playing."

As it was Saints won at a canter – 48-10 – with the sacking of Millward taking much of the sting out of the encounter with bottom placed Wigan strolling out with an armful of excuses – no coach, seven players injured or suspended, the wrong sort of sunshine and undoubtedly a few Wigan fans were probably still chunnering about the salary cap.

As a result Saints were on a bit of a hiding to nothing, particularly after setting a high benchmark of 75-0 the previous summer in that famous Challenge Cup whitewashing. Remarkably it was Saints' first Good Friday win over Wigan since April 2000 – but despite a 38 point winning margin the 17,500 sell-out crowd still seemed subdued and walked away with a sense of anti-climax. Who would have thought that fans could ever have those feelings, in those dark, dismal days of the late 80s and early 90s when the Cherry and Whites were top dogs and Saints could not buy a derby win.

When Saints played simple football they invariably scored with skipper Paul Sculthorpe starting the ball rolling with a try from a Keiron Cunningham pass. Jamie Lyon showed his class to fashion the next one for Paul Wellens before half backs Leon Pryce and Sean Long combined for the latter to bag Saints' third to make it 18-0 at the break. Saints grabbed five more tries in the second half and then started thinking about their early flights to Perpignan the following morning. Saints were definitely dealt the smelly end of the stick by getting Catalans away in the middle of Easter – but they dealt with it.

Saints triumphed 34-20 against the Dragons, with Vinnie Anderson grabbing a well-taken brace of scores, making it two down and one to go in rugby league's equivalent of a triathlon. It was achieved at the cost of losing Mike Bennett with a shoulder injury that would rule him out until late summer. Mindful of the intense three games in eight days schedule, coach Daniel Anderson omitted Paul Sculthorpe, Jason Hooper and Paul Anderson for the game in France.

All three returned for the game against the Reds, as did Ade Gardner, who did not travel to France because his partner was due to give birth to their first child.

Anderson explained: "Three games in eight days is quite a gruelling schedule. The players will focus on the game at hand, but the coaching staff will have to think ahead and schedule their recovery and recuperation and find every opportunity to train and prepare. The boys that are playing in all three games will be going on autopilot."

Speaking before a ball had even been kicked in the Good Friday tussle, Anderson was not the first Australian coach to scratch his head and talk about the stresses and strains placed on the squad over the Easter period, with this one having the extra burden of a flight to the south of France factored in.

"As far as coaching staff are concerned strategically we have to prepare now for the Catalans and Salford games because we just won't have time. We have just one 45 minute training session between the Catalans game and the Salford match. The next seven days is a daunting prospect.

"There are six competition points up for grabs and the league table can change drastically in the space of eight days," Anderson said.

Salford City Reds had blown hot and cold in their time in the top flight – admittedly it was mostly cold but they were nevertheless capable of pulling out a big performance against their rivals Saints, Wigan and Warrington from up the East Lancashire Road. Not that St Helens was on the Red Rose county radar for those Reds choristers packed at the back of the terracing near to the tunnel, who relished the opportunity to spit the words 'scousers'. The Willows was never the most hospitable of grounds – less so in its latter years when it became increasingly dilapidated inside and prone to street crime outside.

Salford were going well in 2006, then occupying fourth place and earning the tag of the season's surprise package. Saints, with just one session under their belts since getting back from France, were presented with something of a banana skin.

And they had to pull out a real backs-to-the-wall 80 minute defensive stint to maintain their 100 per cent start to the season with a 12-10 triumph.

Nothing epitomised that tenacious tackling display more than the sight of James Graham spectacularly smashing the strong running Gareth Haggerty to the ground two minutes from time as the rampant Reds pounded the Saints line for one final onslaught.

What preceded it had been an unbelievable tackling stint, with Saints on autopilot as they stretched a wall of muscle and bone to repel wave after wave of Salford attacks. After tries from Jason Hooper and Ian Hardman, Saints only score after the break was a penalty which proved to be the difference between the sides.

Anderson said: "It was very tough – but that was a culmination of a difficult spell of three games in eight days. That was a very daunting programme – and the fact that St Helens and Hull were the only two sides to emerge with three wins shows just how difficult the schedule is and how hard it is to stay focused.

"Super League is a tough competition this year and we are just finding that opposition teams are wanting to have a crack at St Helens, particularly because we are unbeaten, and that we are not getting much respite. In some games last year we found some teams just were not there to play and were there for the taking and could blow out the second half.

"This year we are finding that every week the opposition is up for it and having a crack for the full 80 minutes and giving us no respite. Our defensive effort was absolutely tremendous at Salford – and although we did spill some ball, much of that was down to mental fatigue.

"It affected our concentration levels and decision-making, but I cannot fault the players' commitment, desire and attitude. I was delighted with their performance. The week was a test of character for us – although it is not something I would like us to have to do again. We knew it would pan out that way because of our inability to play expansive football because we were that tired. I hope we won't have to make that many tackles again!

"Winning can be a habit, but one that is borne out of pride and performance. There is a real sense of pride among the players to deny the opposition any reward. On Friday – it was a really gutsy effort to stop Salford getting anything from that game."

One of the benefits of the strength in depth Saints had in their squad was that it allowed the coach the luxury of resting players who needed one – if only to give them a kick up the backside. Forwards Maurie Fa'asavalu and Jon Wilkin dropped out of the side. Anderson explained: "Both players were sending me signals through their play that they were fatiguing and their form was tapering a little bit and hence this is the reason they were rested. I want them to really freshen up both mentally and physically and then hopefully I will then be able to send another couple of players out for a rest. Injuries permitting, that is our objective in order to freshen up our squad.

"The players are proud and want to play in every game – even though they know the benefits of having a week off."

So it was so far, so good and with 12 wins from 12 matches inevitably there was media speculation centring – sparked by former Knowsley Road coach Ian Millward – on whether Saints could do the unthinkable and go through the season unbeaten. But Anderson was not getting swept away by the media hype, responding in his usual no-nonsense manner.

He said: "It gives the press something to write about until we drop one and then we won't have to talk about it any more! We will have to play well every game for that (winning every game) to happen. As league leaders we are a bit of a target, everyone is chasing us and after our scalp, which makes every game a tough one. We have not had any games where teams have given up late in the game – they relax a little bit against other sides, not against us."

In the aftermath of the Easter programme Anderson had sent his players home from training because they were still shattered. He explained: "I had to can the session on Monday because they were exhausted. They did some weights in the morning, but when they went out on to the field in the afternoon they were listless and there was no quality so we wrapped it up. They have been told to turn up with plenty of energy and no whingeing on Wednesday and I'm sure they will be right."

Whether fatigue was a factor – maybe expectations were so sky high – but even a 34-8 win against Wakefield, one of their regular bogey sides was greeted with a disappointed shrug of the shoulders from fans, players and coach.

It was not the margin of victory that was criticised, more the lethargic, error-strewn, impatient performance which provided poor fare for Saints' first five-figure crowd against Trinity since 1967. Victory was Saints' 13th of the season but Anderson was a far from happy coach.

"We fell a fair way short of how we want to play. In the first half it was ridiculous that we coughed up so much ball. I think we can play a much more mature and professional game when things don't go our way. We just gave them too much possession. Everyone had good bits, but there is more to work on this week than there was at the start of the season. We need to start building again to work our way back into the competition. This year we have gone to the top of our form and have come back down – now we need to build it back up again," he said.

However, one player not in need of pep talk or pick me up was 20-year-old former Blackbrook Royals and Crusaders prop James Graham. It was early days, but a string of consistently impressive performances marked Jammer out as one of the form packmen of Super League. It was not simply his toughness, big heart and bottle – he knew where to run.

Anderson said: "James is a great prospect and puts himself in the right position. He is in Great Britain form. If you named the top four form British props in Super League I would be very surprised if his name was not among them."

Despite being so young for a front rower, Graham's solid, no-nonsense, hard, yard-making and tough tackling were a strong feature of Saints' impressive start to the season.

9

Jason Hooper – the Unsung Nuts and Bolts Man

Saints' all-action Aussie Jason Hooper probably won't find himself on many Christmas card lists of opponents following his stint at Knowsley Road. He was a nitty-gritty, nuts and bolts sort of player who did the ugly bits to enable those with the silky skills to strut their stuff.

With little thought for life and limb, Hooper would be the man to fly in and give an uncomfortable ride to opposing kickers. It may not have won him many friends among opposing players and fans, but it certainly did much to ensure Saints won little battles on field position in crucial games.

Although he came to England as a six, his durability and toughness meant that he played his best rugby at Saints when he took the 13 jersey from in and out skipper Paul Sculthorpe. He was nudged out of the number six shirt he had worn for the three previous years by the signing of Leon Pryce, and then nearly lost his quota spot but Hooper approached that season upbeat about the challenges facing him for the year ahead.

Talking in pre-season, after he had been told that he would be 'utility' in 2006, Hooper did not take that as a demotion. With enthusiasm he said: "You can play different roles each week – I may not be starting every week – but as long as I am in the 17 I'll be happy.

"I have set myself a couple of goals for next year – get my 100th game for the club, start as many games as I can and hopefully win some trophies."

The truth is the former St George-Illawarra player, then aged

28, was just pleased to still be wearing the red vee after a miserable year with injuries and the very real prospect at one stage that he had played his last game for Saints.

Hooper said: "Parts of 2005 were just terrible. I don't think I have ever had a season so bad, missing the first ten weeks with my knee. The operation went totally wrong and then when I returned to the fold I was just about getting some good form on the board when I dislocated my shoulder – three times. People have those sorts of seasons, you just have to bounce back from them."

The last of those injuries was most worrying for Hooper and was sustained during Saints' 75-0 thrashing of Wigan in the cup game. The smiles all round Knowsley Road that day were not matched by the grimace on Hooper's face, particularly as it had just been announced there was no room for him on Saints' overseas quota with big prop Jason Cayless coming in from Sydney Roosters.

He said: "It wasn't that I wasn't playing well or anything like that, it was just that there was no quota space because they needed a front rower. When I came off – even though I had received offers from elsewhere – all I kept thinking was that I had played my last game for Saints.

"I was lucky that my shoulder was not as bad as I thought and I was able to play six weeks later, but at the time I thought of not having a contract and being unable to press for one with a dislocated shoulder was pretty tough."

He was lined up for Salford, who had made the versatile Aussie a lucrative offer to join them at the Willows. But then he was presented with a choice when he was given a nod from compatriot Darren Albert, who was keen to take up an offer in Sydney.

"Darren said to me 'don't sign for anybody else yet because I am going to ask for a release to go to Cronulla' so when that went through I spoke to Eamonn and Daniel and it really fell back into place.

"I bought Albie a couple of beers afterwards, that is for sure. I always wanted to stay – and am so glad it turned out that way, especially looking at the squad we had."

Coach Daniel Anderson got great value from Hooper for the team – and he was classed as one of those selfless players that did a lot of the unfashionable stuff that rarely grabbed a headline.

During that season Anderson said: "It has been quite a year for Jason, who looked set to be leaving the club. We had made a commitment last year that Leon Pryce would wear number six and that meant Hoops was not going to be our first choice stand off. With quota players you have to be more diligent how you use those spots.

"But Jason is a very popular player, people enjoy playing alongside him because he is selfless and does the jobs nobody likes doing. We brought him back for a year and he 'stumbled' into the loose forward position in the early part of the off-season. He has done so much that he cannot be moved and is now our first choice loose forward.

"I gave Jason the option to do what he did in the NRL and play in the back row. He has put on four or five kilos and is playing 13 now and is all over the field. His forte is always going to be running the ball and supporting players and is very comfortable in that job.

"Although every player has their own assets, he does things for us that other players do not."

Speaking to Hooper just ahead of the Challenge Cup Final – his second for the Saints – he talked about his role, which caused a few raised eyebrows when skipper Sculthorpe moved to accommodate him

"I have been a bit more consistent this year with the things I am doing and Daniel has given me a role to do. I have not necessarily pushed Scully out, it is just that the coach has given him a different running role. My game is different – I just try and tidy up, push up, chase and put pressure on the kicker. They are just little things that sometimes get overlooked," he said.

It was not all plain sailing and Hooper had to modify his charge on the kicker after he was sin-binned twice in consecutive weeks earlier in the year and was rapidly being turned into the game's bad boy.

"I don't think kickers like playing against me and I have copped a bit of abuse this season. I was sin-binned two weeks in a row – so I sat down with Daniel and he has helped change my technique a bit. It has come good since then and I've had no trouble," he said.

His technique might have had to subtly change over the course of that year, but he nevertheless still possessed that dogged 'run through a brick wall' style that made him a formidable if not flashy performer.

Speaking some seven years later, Saints' full back Paul Wellens, who had a great view of Hooper in action listed the pugnacious Aussie as one of the club's most valuable players. Wellens declared: "Jason Hooper was one of those players who, when you met up with other clubs' players on international duty, they would all hate him. They would say things like 'he is a grub,' 'he is this, that and the other' – but he was one of those players that you loved playing alongside.

"He would run lines and get whacked and would get up and say 'I am not bothered'. He was as tough as they come. He came originally as a six so had good hands and we all saw that in the lead up to Willie Talau's try in the Grand Final. But he preferred back row – so in a way when Leon came that was his big chance.

"Another thing was that he was probably one of the fittest blokes in the team. He was a flying machine in training and it was only towards the back end of his career at Saints, when he kept getting his injuries with his knee, that it affected him.

"He looked like he was on his way before that year started – but Darren Albert went back to Australia and that meant we could keep Hoops. Looking back it could have been a different year without Jason – but you would have to ask Lee Briers about Jason. I have spoken to him a few times and he has said 'I hated that guy' because he literally mithered the life out of him for 80 minutes." Indeed, it may be urban myth but there is a story doing the rounds saying when Hooper cracked Briers early on in the game in March. Briers was supposed to have said "That was nothing." To which the yarn goes, "That's good then, you are going to be feeling nothing for another 75 minutes!"

10

May

It was all going well but the quirks of the 'extra' fixtures threw up a second trip to Huddersfield for Saints' 13th Super League game of the campaign. Although Giants had lost their previous five games and the form book said an easy Saints win, the 19-16 loss at the Galpharm Stadium was exactly what the depleted side deserved.

With Jason Cayless in Brisbane for the ANZAC Test, Jamie Lyon out with an eye infection, Lee Gilmour sidelined with a hip injury, Sean Long 'rested' and Keiron Cunningham and Leon Pryce occupying seats on the bench it was a game that tested Saints much trumpeted strength in depth. And on this occasion – for the first time of the season – they were found wanting.

Saints possibly underestimated their more enthusiastic and desperate opponents and got their just desserts with the one-man rugby being poor fare for the 2,000 travelling fans. As poorly as Saints played, the result was a close-run thing and had it gone on for a further five minutes the momentum was tipping Saints' way after the fired-up James Graham had charged over for a try.

But the best team won with disjointed Saints being a pale shadow of the side that had blasted away all-comers so far that season. Saints started with two teenagers at half back in Matty Smith and Scott Moore, with James Roby handed a rare starting role.

But there were other factors at play than this one game – the bigger picture balancing act of rotating a squad that had been showing signs of fatigue, was explained by Anderson.

He said: "We don't like to lose and certainly don't prepare to lose a game, but we were beaten by a more enthusiastic team on the day. We do not have to rewrite the book, our formula is solid, but we simply have to work harder.

"Questions have been asked about the absence of Sean Long, and my decision to start Keiron Cunningham and Leon Pryce on the bench. It is a bit of a myth to say that Longy was rested. Although mentally he didn't have to get ready for a game, physically he had to train even harder. The players start off the year with a really big base built up as a result of an off-season training programme. However, as the weeks go by – because of the games and the Easter period – they don't train as much and start to lose that base. I think our players have lost a bit of fitness and strength.

"So that is one reason behind those selection decisions.

"Added to that we have a massive game against Bradford next week, which would have been Longy's 16th in a row. It is very hard to hold your physical strength and endurance for 16 weeks. So last week he went out and trained harder than every bloke who played, and he is buzzing at the moment. Sean will play for another big spell, depending on injury, but if I feel he needs another period where he needs to train instead of play, then we will do that.

"The third aspect is that we need to know where we stand with our squad, especially those players who don't play that much. We lost Sean Long for the play-off games last year and then had to throw Scott Moore in at the deep end.

"Keiron and Leon started on the bench because I have to try and give our players more respite. It is important to keep in perspective that we are just past the third month of a nine-month competition, and we still have plenty of weeks to play."

It was important that Saints, at this stage struggling with injuries, got back on the horse quickly against an in-form Warrington. Long-term casualties Maurie Fa'asavalu, who was ruled out with torn knee ligaments, and Mike Bennett, sidelined until the first week of September having undergone an operation on his damaged shoulder were joined by Paul Wellens, Paul Anderson, Francis Meli and Willie Talau.

This was a game that Wolves, seeking their first summer era win at Knowsley Road, would have targeted. In later years, when he was boss of Widnes, Paul Cullen revealed how much physically and emotionally Wire invested in trying to break that Saints hoodoo. With each last-gasp defeat those scars became deeper and their desire to overcome them intensified.

So Wolves would again have been licking their lips on the sly for this one. But any hints of a Saints' vulnerability was overcome with a blistering three-try spell in the nine crucial minutes before the break to help return Saints to winning ways – 34-22.

After rattling up a 26-4 interval lead they withstood a ferocious second half rally, which saw their lead whittled down to four points. A Jamie Lyon penalty six minutes from time gave them a six point cushion, but Wolves still pressed the line.

The game was on a knife-edge but in Wolves' haste to breach the line one last time Stuart Reardon pushed one pass too many for Ade Gardner to intercept and race 80-metres to score. Seeing a Saints number two fly in from long range no doubt delighted Tom van Vollenhoven, who was watching from the stands.

He was not the only one happy with boss Daniel Anderson expressing his satisfaction when interviewed after the match.

"I was really proud of the performance. Sometimes you have to look into the mirror when things don't go your way. I don't think we have played well as a team for a few weeks. We got stung last week, but tonight was a great team performance," he said.

"After the previous week's disruption – caused by a number of injuries and losing a day because of the GB training camp – it was pleasing to turn out such a good team performance.

"Many players were asked to play out of position due to injuries that hit the team prior to kick off. One was Ade Gardner. Ade took his closing try very well and his overall performance was pleasing. I asked him to switch wings to mark Henry Fa'afili, a player who has scored a lot of his tries from the air.

"When it comes to dealing with high balls I believe Ade is defensively the most accomplished wingman in Super League. Ade's decision making has improved markedly and his overall play reflects maturity. The opportunity to represent his country can only be enhanced by quality play in big games like this Saturday.

"We have big wingers and they caused Warrington a few

73

problems in the air when attacking Sean Long's kicks. It does not matter how good your opponent is – if you compete in the air with vigour and enthusiasm you are likely to make your own luck.

"Sean's kicking to our wingmen has been the result of hours of practice and it is a real string to his bow."

Saints had had an eye on the Challenge Cup clash against Bradford for the previous fortnight – and that had clearly influenced the coach's selection policy who revealed that some of the previous week's absentees could have played. It probably showed the determination of Saints' leadership – from chairman, coach, staff and leading players – to focus on bringing home that first piece of silverware.

Although Bradford Bulls have suffered something of a spectacular fall from grace in recent times, back in 2006 they were the reigning champions and earlier that year had been good enough to beat Wests Tigers in the World Club Challenge. Before the rise of Leeds, the Bulls were arguably the team that had given Saints the biggest run for their money in the early years of Super League. Champions in 1997, 2001 and 2003, an Adrian Morley-inspired Bulls had been the previous year's juggernaut storming to the title from third.

Moz was back with the Roosters, Jamie Peacock had joined the Rhinos and coach Brian Noble had decamped to the JJB in May to try and save Wigan from relegation, leading to future England boss Steve McNamara taking the helm. The omens were with Saints – especially since renowned match winner Leon Pryce had swapped the amber and black of his home town for the red vee.

Bradford had traditionally been good Challenge Cup opponents for Saints – with three cup final successes coming against the Bulls in 1996, 1997 and 2001. In fact, the last time Saints had lost a Challenge Cup tie against Bradford was by a single point margin back in 1980 when the visitors were still plain old Northern.

Anderson said: "St Helens have a rich tradition of going well in the Challenge Cup and we are not aiming to end that this Saturday. But we face very tough opposition who have come back to form in the last couple of weeks."

It was not that tough and the World Club champions were

made to look distinctly ordinary after being taken apart by clinical Saints' power, pace and skill winning 42-18. Although a close tie had been anticipated, Saints had their quarter-final passage booked by half-time after using the strong wind to rack up an unassailable 26-6 first half lead.

Bradford were never allowed so much as a toe hold in the game, such was the enthusiasm Saints showed in meeting their ball carriers head on with the Popular Side revelling in the sight of big men like Lesley Vainikolo and Stuart Fielden being carted backwards by the ferocity of Saints' tackling.

After something of a minor blip in the previous weeks, Saints hit top gear with Sean Long pulling the strings with an exemplary kicking display. His grubbers, chips and cross kicks constantly caused all kinds of problems for the Bulls defence and helped keep play at the right end of the field. The platform for Long to operate so effectively was created by the industry of Saints' front row with Paul Anderson and Jason Cayless making hard, quick yards and at their heels Keiron Cunningham was able to keep the Bulls defence back-pedalling as he threaded his way through from dummy half.

Cunningham completely bossed the ruck area and was rewarded with a brace of tries including Saints' second minute settler, which came from brute force close to the line, the second a combination of poise, vision and strength in the way he was able to spot the deficiencies in an increasingly disinterested Bulls defence to thread his way through the split markers at the play-the-ball then brush off Deacon's challenge to touch down.

Saints' front row gave the Bulls a taste of their own medicine. Not so many moons prior to that year Bradford had boasted an 'awesome foursome' of rotated big props. But one of that quartet, Anderson was thriving in the Indian summer he enjoyed in Saints colours – and relished combat against a Bulls club that had put him out to pasture.

Cayless, an often overlooked component of the team that year, gave so much to the midfield. Although injuries derailed subsequent seasons in the red vee, in 2006 he was immense – and a real Steady Eddie when the bullets were flying in the opening 20 minutes. Strong and quick, the lanky Kiwi Test prop used his tall frame to engage defenders and wriggle his long arms free to get the ball away. It was such a ploy that resulted in Saints sniffer Paul Wellens snaffling a try that afternoon against Bradford.

When the first roster of props had done their bit, the late shift of James Graham and Nick Fozzard took over.

Anderson remarked: "We were just ferocious from the first minute to the last and just wanted to be in their faces, be aggressive and dominate the space on the field.

"We were really powerful – Keiron Cunningham was outstanding in the thick of the action and Longy's kicking game was tremendous. Our senior players like Scully, Paul Wellens, Paul Anderson – our old hard heads if you like – stood up and led the way.

"Everyone contributed to the victory – I cannot find a bloke who did not make a huge contribution, I could list them all, from one to 17."

And so with that resounding win, Daniel Anderson's men bounced into their next game and the contrast between the fortunes of high-flying Saints, then six points clear at the top, and those of a Wigan side, then staring into the abyss at the foot of the table, could not have been starker. How the times had changed.

It would have been hard, nay, impossible to have ever envisaged that state of affairs in those dark days between 1988 and 1995 when the Cherry and Whites swept all before them at a packed Central Park. Although the Warriors had, up to that point, won one Grand Final and one Challenge Cup since ditching the Riversiders tag for the Warriors moniker, it was clear that despite sitting on a pool of raw talent and splashing the cash Wigan had never really come to terms with the concept of a level playing field. They later would, but it would take the massive convulsions they went through in 2006 to shock their system and eventually get it right.

When the two rivals from either side of Billinge Lump met that May, Saints were clear top with Warriors anchored to the foot of the table in 12th – a position they had occupied since March.

The first part of Wigan's prescription to dodge the drop had been to bring in Brian Noble from the Bulls, who then enticed former Saints full back Phil Veivers over as his assistant. But a key component of their survival bid was bringing in 19-year-old Canberra Raiders scrum half Michael Dobson, who had been on loan at Catalan, and sending Dennis Moran out to Widnes. Dobson was thrown in at the deep end against Saints.

That said, derby matches had a habit of throwing up an unknown ingredient – and Wigan were hungry and desperate to breathe life into their dismal 2006 campaign so Saints were on the guard although Anderson clearly had a focus on the Challenge Cup game the week later.

He said: "All my focus is on the game versus Wigan followed by the game against Catalan. I am not worried about what the opposition think, I am going to do what is best for our club. Wigan will be quite a desperate team, but we are going ok and have a lot of players who are in form. There is also plenty of competition for spots.

"I expect Wigan to raise their game, especially as they are at home, and don't expect them to be anything but wound up. Once again I am looking at a two-week sequence of games with an eye on the cup.

"That does not mean I am giving up the game to Wigan and am not sending out a B-grade team. It is a derby game after all and the players are very proud of the jersey they wear and are very aware that we can continue to put the foot on the throat of Wigan."

And so it was with Sean Long triumphantly returning to the Wigan ground where his season was so brutally shattered the previous season, ignoring a hostile response from the boo-boys in the home section and a few bruising tackles to turn in a match winning performance.

Although there had been strong hints in the build up that Long would sit out the last Wigan derby of the year to preserve him for the following weekend's cup tie, there were a few relieved smiles among Saints fans when the team sheet was read out. And the durable half back certainly showed no ill-effects of any knocks he may have been carrying, picking up where he left off the previous week with another man of the match performance.

Relegation-haunted Wigan, buoyed by the arrival of Dobson,

significantly raised their game and had the lion's share of territorial advantage in the first half but Saints eased home 28-14. The highlight – and subsequent You Tube sensation – was second rower Vinnie Anderson rattling Danny Tickle with a bone-crunching tackle that reverberated around the ground and left the Wigan packman creased double in agony from the copybook head-on tackle.

Daniel said: "Vinnie's hit was a very strong tackle and we had a look at it in the video review session on Monday. It certainly made good television, but we can only guess what Vinnie said after the tackle when the adrenalin was pumping!

"Since I have been at Saints everyone has told me the importance of beating Wigan, and it was good to carry on that winning record – and hopefully we are doing the fans proud on that score. We are playing with a level of composure that goes with a side that is playing well. We are not rushing things or over-cooking it – we are happy to wait for things to fall for us, which is a sign of a team in form."

As for Wigan's relegation, it never happened. The signing of Stuart Fielden from Bradford for a world record fee of £450,000 helped solidify the pack even if it did contribute to them committing the biggest salary cap breach in the Super League's history – busting the limit of £1.6m on payments by £222,314. They were docked four points the following season in 2007 despite a defence which included a claim that nine senior players had agreed to go without wages for the last three months of the season.

11

Cunningham and Roby – the Twin Track Threat of Master and Apprentice

The statue above Saints' new Langtree Park home shows any visitors the high esteem Keiron Cunningham is held in St Helens. Bizarrely, the one-man bulldozer and master at calling the shots from dummy half never picked up any of the individual awards during his long, illustrious and trophy-laden career but when it was put to the public vote in his home town he won hands down.

Keiron Cunningham, King Keiron, Kez, the local hero from Thatto Heath was simply immense. And although it is true he turned his job into shift work, it was always two devastating stints of the highest quality that he contributed.

And to make Cunningham's shifts even more effective Saints had a Plan B in former Blackbrook Royals junior James Roby, who was thrown on after 30 minutes to provide the perfect contrast. So once teams had just about got used to trying, and invariably failing, to combat Cunningham's sheer physical presence they then had to come to terms with Roby's rapier like thrusts from dummy half. It made for the perfect twin track approach and Saints' offence was always on the front foot.

That they were operating at the heels of a big front row that was able to marmalise the opposition and put them on the front foot, and that the pair could link with an experienced seven in Sean Long and an on-song full back in the attacking spine helped matters, but Saints' hookers deserved all the plaudits they got in 2006.

Significantly, Daniel Anderson's commitment to playing Cunningham nowhere else but nine was a significant first decision and it was repaid tenfold.

Anderson said: "I made some minor tweaks first day I got here I spoke to Keiron and told him you will never play any position apart from hooker in a team that I coach.

"He was the best hooker in the world in my opinion, and I was aware that he had been playing like a front rower. I told others would move to suit him. I am pretty sure I lived up to that but he repaid me in spades."

When Keiron charged from dummy half close to line it invariably parted and it usually involved opposing colours flying up in the air or left in a crumpled heap on the floor.

But that was only a fraction of his game offensively. Cunningham's skill was that he could take the punishment of a boxing ring, be toe-to-toe with the hardest men in the middle and take the clouts around his lug hole and inject his own physicality, and in the next split second still make the decisions of a chess master. He was the personification of Mike Tyson and Garry Kasparov and his precise delivery from dummy half launched more or less every big play.

Anderson rated him as a decision maker out of the top drawer of world rugby league. That expertise came from Cunningham spending all his years since late teens in the Saints nine shirt. And although with the ball he would rumble over the opposition like a human wrecking ball, defensively he could spearhead some really punishing defence. He would whack them, meet them head on, cut them in half with pure brute force and send them reeling backwards.

It was a two-spell job for a reason, those 80 minutes of a normal shift were distilled and condensed into two intense contributions. Cunningham was the ultimate warrior, one who tended to shun press conferences, and talking publicly about his talents – the talking was done on the pitch.

When looking at Cunningham, not just in 2006, but every subsequent season in the red vee culminating in his curtain call last days of Knowsley Road performances, you have to ask yourself how come so many rugby 'experts' got it so wrong. For after he had badly dislocated his elbow playing for Great Britain against New Zealand in 2002 it genuinely was a career-threatening injury. He missed three months at the start of 2003 season and there were plenty who thought he would never be the same player. That culminated with Millward playing him at 'roving go forward,' a euphemism for front row if ever there was one, once nippy impact number nine Mickey Higham had been thrown into the fray.

But from the 2005/06 seasons, Cunningham was able to give as much quality to his last five as he had to his first half a dozen in the red vee. Although he did not have the same pace that saw him race 50 metres for a try in the Challenge Cup semi-final against Salford in 1997 or that length of the field chase back to nail Mark Smith at Easter 2002 – he made up for that loss of a yard with that extra bit of nous.

Speaking at the end of 2013, Saints skipper Paul Wellens, who watched Cunningham in full flow, felt that he now had an even greater insight on the contribution made by the former number nine after a season of swapping the last line of defence for a spell on the front line.

He said: "It is only since I started defending in that middle line that I started thinking Keiron has been doing that all of his career. Even though I had a huge amount of respect for Keiron, I think I have even more so now that I have actually walked a mile in his shoes.

"First of all his presence alone on the field was worth ten points to us. Even if you talk about those last games at Knowsley Road and Keiron came striding on and it had an immediate effect.

"Nor can you underestimate how good a rugby player he actually was. He kind of did a great deal of things that at the time we never saw but now that he has gone me and Wilko will talk to each other and ask 'why is X no longer happening on the field?' and we will both arrive at the conclusion that 'Keiron did that'.

"Keiron would never bang his drum and say 'I do this and that', but he was just a very smart rugby player. You don't replace a player like Keiron and it only hit home after he had gone how much he was doing."

But looking back to the mid-noughties, Wellens recalls how the changeover at coaching level re-affirmed Cunningham as the best number nine in the British game and in 2005 and 2006 he was reinstated to the Dream Team after a two year break when the fictitious crown was handed to Matt Diskin and Terry Newton.

"When Ian Millward was coach, there was a huge pressure to accommodate Mickey Higham. Ian at the time had this idea of Keiron playing what was classed as 'roving go forward'. Keiron was going mental, and I used to wind him up at the time and say 'that means prop you know.' It is funny this year (2013) when I got asked to play up in the middle with the forwards Keiron nodded to me 'roving go forward' and I knew it had come full circle.

"Keiron would have done anything for the team but Daniel knew he was the best nine in the world. Mickey is a great player but Daniel made the decision to move him on because he had seen this lad James Roby who was more suited to nine. As far as master strokes go, the decision is right up there."

A young forward in 2006, one who made it his job to support up the middle, Jon Wilkin prospered from following Cunningham. Wilkin saw at first-hand how brutally devastating that twin track dummy half approach was in demoralising and defeating opposing defences.

Wilkin said: "We had Keiron and James at dummy half and we built our game around blowing teams away in the middle of the field. I think there is an idea for maintaining that strategy. Some of the best teams of the moment (in 2013) are spelling their two nines in the game. We did it better than anyone in the noughties.

"Keiron was absolutely immense, he was unbelievable. His stats were tremendous at Twickenham when we won the cup and we had a couple of guys in the team who played the ball really quickly so my job was to follow Keiron around. I had a great understanding with him. Keiron changed the role of hooker single handed.

"It always amuses me that Keiron could play so well in so many big games and yet not get near a sniff of an individual accolade. He was amazing that day – if you look back and watch the game and his contribution was incredible. It is hard to understand how he did not got the man of the match – I know me and Sean Long were in the running for the Lance Todd in 2006 at Twickenham but Keiron should have been well up there. I find the whole lack of awards for him bizarre – maybe Keiron is just a victim around that time of his consistent high quality performances being the norm."

Understudy – if that is not too insulting a term – Roby was also an integral part of the way Saints utterly bamboozled the opposition in 2006. Then aged just 20, Roby was in his first full season as an established player – and although most teams had now become aware of the former Blackbrook junior's toolkit, combating that was a different matter, particularly in that ten minute spell before half-time when tiring bodies were hanging on for that bell.

Roby recalls: "When they let Mickey go and I kind of took his place as Keiron's understudy – working in tandem with Keiron. It was obviously a great deal for myself with Mickey being such an experienced hooker, and having played for Great Britain. For Daniel Anderson to have faith in me and say 'I want you to do that, you can do just as good a job' then I was made up.

"Playing in a squad like we had back then was immense, we just had that much talent that we were always confident. There were certain games that we turned up and we knew we were going to win. It was great to be involved in a team like that.

"And not in a bad way, we had a lot of egos as well – there were a lot of big name stars in the team that had that about them but that probably helped our image. As young lads me and James Graham were pretty quiet. Jammer still is quiet unless you get him angry – and we just kind of went along with everything and did what the coach told us. We were very lucky to come through into a team of such quality – and we won all those honours. It was great for us as players and I don't think it is any coincidence that it made us better by playing with such good experienced players in our early days."

The double act with Cunningham was a key weapon, but Roby was always indebted to his predecessor's contribution in the brutal, muck or nettles opening quarter of the games.

"It worked perfectly well. Keiron, with his size and his

experience, would go on for that first 20 minutes. That period of any game is where all the emotion gets you and a few big hits are flying in as you wear each other down. Then, after Keiron has whacked a few of theirs and bore the brunt of what they have thrown back in return I would obviously come on then and I'd be young and fresh.

"I got told to run as much as I could and try and create a bit of a spark around the middle. When you have some big lads who have been playing for 20 or 30 minutes solid and a small lad comes on who can use a bit of footwork, some of them struggled. I got the rewards with the breaks and tries and looking good but Keiron had been on before me and done all that hard work for me. It seemed to work fantastic and we won all those trophies."

2006 was Boy's Own stuff for Roby and Graham – and both were rewarded by international call-ups. But the first real landmark game was the Challenge Cup Final – his first senior medal as a professional.

"Everything seemed to fall in place for us that season," Roby said.

"Twickenham was good because it was my first taste of winning something and a Challenge Cup final is such a massive occasion. The whole build up was good – there was always a buzz about it, that was a great event to be involved with. I was made up with winning the cup with Saints and felt lucky I had come into the team that year and secured my place. It gave us confidence and we had that about us."

"You take it for granted that you are going to win stuff, when everything is going right. The last few years make you realise that you can't take anything for granted especially when all the other teams are getting better – you have to up your game to stay in the position you are. At St Helens trophies are expected but that is a good thing, perform or the fans are going to be on your backs. We hope to turn that around and get something with our names on this next couple of years."

Roby has had that illustrious number nine jersey since Cunningham hung up his boots at the end of the Knowsley Road era. They have proven to be big boots to fill, being the starting hooker and unlike the noughties he is putting in regular 80 minute shifts. Cunningham, however, is still a positive influence and passes on his pearls of wisdom as assistant coach to Nathan Brown.

It is an influence Roby has been glad of over the years and the adulation, admiration and respect that greeted the uncrowned King of Thatto Heath when he bowed out in 2010 motivates rather than over-awes him.

"Keiron has been a big influence on my career – I can't quantify it, but he was there all the time as a player and then became my coach. I picked up a lot of stuff off him when I was younger," Roby said.

"We were different styles, with different traits and different strengths. It also helped me that Keiron was such a great player and loved by the fans and that made me want to be more like that. That made me try harder, the competitiveness helped me out.

"Nowadays, as coach, he does a lot of work with our attack and one on one stuff with the forwards. I like the way he goes about his coaching. He tells it how it is and there is no nonsense. He will tell you what to do – he is straight up and down and that suits me."

12

June

June started off as planned when the strategy of rotating the squad saw a refreshed Saints rattle in ten tries past Catalans to cruise into a sixth successive Challenge Cup semi-final. Not even the return of veteran half Stacey Jones, the man who had guided the Kiwis to a shock Tri-Nations Series win over Australia in 2005, could help save the Dragons from the sword.

That said, the talismanic number seven showed no sign of ring rustiness when he did what he had been doing for a decade, showing and going before bisecting Paul Wellens and Paul Anderson to give his side a 6-4 lead.

However, there was simply no holding Saints once they got their noses back in front with Ade Gardner's hat-trick being the highlight of the half century mauling. The Barrow Arrow, who was on fire that year, would have got a fourth had he not spilled the ball over the line after inter-passing with Sean Long from deep inside his own half.

Despite the treble Gardner was self critical afterwards, declaring: "You have to be tough on yourself. Sometimes the bounce of the ball just does not go your way, but despite scoring three tries, making a few breaks and chasing a couple of players down in the match I was still really down about it.

"You always remember the bad things you do and the silly errors that sometimes happen in games. With that lost ball over the line – I did not really drop it, I was just complacent and the tackler knocked it out.

"With being a winger those errors can be magnified. If someone misses a tackle in the middle you don't always notice it, but wingers and full backs are exposed."

Nobody else was really losing any sleep over that error from the wingman as the game meandered to a conclusion. The blistering heat, complete absence of away fans among the five-figure crowd, ease of victory and the frequent stoppages gave the match the atmosphere of a pre-season run out.

With the place in the semis booked, the only mildly frustrating aspect was that those Challenge Cup thoughts then had to be put on the backburner until the last week of July.

It was back to bread and butter and June's Super League encounters would provide Saints with something of a reality check, and the first warning as to the likelihood of their biggest rivals for the top prize that term – Hull FC.

Under John Kear, the Black and Whites had been the shock Challenge Cup winners in 2005. But the knowledgeable Yorkshire coach had been shown the door in April a fortnight after Saints had thumped Hull 46-0 for their first win at the KC Stadium.

The arrival of Parramatta assistant Peter Sharp injected some steel into the Humbersiders and so began their push from the fringes of mid-table respectability to leapfrogging three of the other members of the traditional big four – Leeds, Bradford and Wigan.

The Airlie Bird hordes travelled over to Knowsley Road in numbers despite the anti-social Thursday night fixture – an unusual occurrence back then. And they were rewarded by witnessing a pulsating match and going home with their first win at Knowsley Road for 18 years.

After battling back from a 10-point deficit, Saints were sunk by the long-legged Paul Cooke's 40-metre drop goal which went in off the posts. On balance the 27-26 result was a fair reflection with Anderson's mob left to rue taking some poor options and uncharacteristically playing some headless chicken football.

Significantly, Hull man of the match Cooke did not have to worry about Jason Hooper, who missed the game due to his wife giving birth to their third child. Who knows what difference he would have made, if any, in harrying the kicker at the end of the game?

Defeat may have been a blessing in disguise given the fuss made over an earlier substitution error when Saints temporarily had 14-men on the field defending one set of six. It was a minor incident and should in no way overshadow what had been the best game of the season so far. Even in victory the blunt visiting coach Sharp made it clear that Saints would not have kept the points.

It was a match laced with good play and incident. It crackled from the outset, with Nick Fozzard celebrating his new two-year deal at Saints with his first touchdown for 18 months. The big prop showed good pace, determination and a fine hand-off to bash the ball over the line and ensure that he would not have to do any naked run forfeits that year.

When Sean Long scorched over from 40 metres, after good work from Keiron Cunningham, Paul Wellens and Jon Wilkin, Saints had a ten-point lead and looked to be coasting.

But Cooke, displaying the full set of skills of an old school ball player, helped swing the pendulum Hull's way who racked up a ten-point lead ten minutes after the break. That seemed a lost cause for Saints but they were given a glimmer of hope when Lyon twisted out of a tackle to go over at the three quarter mark. Then quick hands allowed Gardner to squeeze in at the corner, with Lyon's touchline conversion making it all square. But as the game entered its frantic closing stages, it was Hull who kept their heads to snatch the spoils. It had been a real roller-coaster of a game a tough loss to take, but may have just been the reminder Saints needed that nothing was a given. It also underlined the view that these two sides would have to meet again at the business end of the season.

Anderson said: "We were up against a team whose effort in defending their own line matched what we normally do. I have some ideas and we need to talk through some minor adjustments we need to make in our game. That said, I cannot fault our boys efforts or their attitude and I thought we did some really good things during the game.

"We need to make those adjustments because teams change through the year – St Helens will change and so will the opposition.

"Neither myself nor the players like losing, but supporters have seen us put a bar up in the first three months of the competition.

They want to see that standard maintained every week – and so do we.

"Let's put the loss into perspective, we have played 19 games this year and won 17 of those, so our goals remain the same. The key objectives are to be in the big games in both competitions. We are in the semi-final of the Challenge Cup in six weeks and we want a top two finish at the end of Super League, if not the League Leaders' Shield to propel us into the play-offs."

Saints' next job was a trip to the champions Bradford, who they had already beaten twice earlier in the year at Knowsley Road, including the Challenge Cup clash.

For coach Daniel Anderson it was about keeping focus in what is traditionally a tough spell, with those big games where the pots were handed out being so far in the distance. Anderson said: "We need to consolidate and prepare for this tough middle part of the year, when the players just cannot see the end of the road."

The Hull defeat was not the end of the world, but that road looked a little tougher after Saints gave away a 10-point lead for the second week running to lose 20-18. Although they failed to get the rub of the green with the referee's calls they only had themselves to blame for letting another game slip through their fingers.

Saints initially appeared to be well on top – and but for some sloppy finishing and a bizarre refereeing decision that gifted the Bulls their first try from a forward pass they would have taken an unassailable lead at the break.

But they failed to add to their score in the second half, crumpling in the face of a determined Bulls' second half performance and a debilitating penalty count. Bradford did nothing special – they simply executed the basics well, completing their sets and kicked well to keep Saints at arm's length.

Saints had fallen behind through a disputed try with Terry Newton's pass out of the tackle going forward to Deacon, who was left with the formality of catching and falling down for a try. The Bulls would have extended that lead but for Paul Wellens' head-on tackle stopping the runaway track that was Lesley Vainikolo in full flight just metres from the line. It was a tackle that was talked about for months afterwards – the Volcano was rarely stopped mid eruption, with most defenders in a one on one situation usually playing the role of speed bumps rather than crash barriers.

It gave Saints the pep-up they needed and Wellens showed his attack was also up to scratch when he polished off fine inter-passing between Long and Nick Fozzard to touch down. When James Graham stormed downfield and sent Gilmour flying in at the corner to make it 18-8 Saints looked odds on to make it their third win of the season over the reigning champions.

But tries from Vainikolo and Deacon's second levelled matters, with the latter stealing it with a penalty when Saints were punished for not being square at the marker.

Anderson said: "For the second week running we have given up a 10-point lead and lost – and it goes without saying that none of us are happy with that. We don't like losing matches as a club or as a dressing room and personally I am a poor loser.

"All credit to Bradford for fighting their way back into the game, but sometimes, when we are going well, we have a tendency to drop our level of intensity. The next thing you know the opposition are back in the game and it is then very hard to find that same gear we had before. Unfortunately, we have been letting teams get a higher level of intensity than us of late, and then fighting back when it is all too late.

"We need to show a bit more desperation and intensity over a longer period of the game, if not the full 80 minutes. If we do that we will be a better team and will win games.

"The penalty count was heavily against us, and our play warranted a number of those decisions. In training on Monday we worked on our tackling technique because we gave too many penalties as a result of high shots.

"However, there were half a dozen penalties that were 50:50 but you deal with those because sometimes they come in your favour. But all you want from a referee is consistency. If he is going to punish us for high shots, grapple tackles and not standing square at the marker then those rules need to be applied as judiciously to the opposition.

"After watching the game I am not pulling my hair out wondering 'what am I going to do?' We are well below what we can be for 20 to 30 minutes of each game. There are plenty more matches this year and we are still in the prime position in the league. But if we are to succeed this year we have to play better than we have done in the last two weeks."

Two defeats on the spin was hardly the best way of heading into what was effectively three games in the next eight days – starting with a tricky home tie against Salford followed by the Great Britain v New Zealand Test match featuring 12 players.

Saints boss Daniel Anderson was confident his dozen international players would remain focused – despite having a big Test on the horizon. He said: "There are distractions in every player's daily make-up, be it the Test match or the cup semi-final in a few weeks and there are also plenty of things off the field that can distract them.

"But for the moments they are in training and on the pitch they have got to focus on the job at hand and let things flow from that. They just have to do the job now."

Explaining why he had dropped James Roby and Maurie Fa'asavalu down to the Academy for the Salford game, Anderson said: "They are both young in their careers and are suffering a bit of a form slump, and James is coming back from his first serious injury.

"He just needs a bit of game time to get a bit of confidence and he will be back in the Super League team very soon. Maurie played 70 minutes in the Academy at the weekend. He too needed to get some minutes under his belt and restore some confidence. He did that!"

Although it was far from their most convincing performance of the year, Saints bounced back to winning ways to beat Salford 28-6. Back-to-back losses had clearly affected the side's confidence, provoking a jittery, impatient first half display against a gutsy Salford. But despite the closeness of the contest at the break, Saints never looked in danger of losing. Once again Saints' pack was dominant, with Keiron Cunningham's play from dummy half prising open the visiting defence on numerous occasions.

The robust number nine had a fine game – and it was noticeable that once again Saints appeared to go off the boil just before the break when Cunningham was off the park. Although Saints got off to a fine start with Leon Pryce powering on to Sean Long's pass to touch down, poor finishing stopped them wrapping the game up.

Test match rugby returned to Knowsley Road for the first time since 1971 – and both the home fans and Saints' eight-strong contingent of players in the GB ranks rose to the occasion.

Great Britain beat a Super League-based New Zealand side 46-14 with scrum half Sean Long and James Graham capping fine games with a brace of tries each, whilst Ade Gardner marked his Test debut with a try in the corner.

But it was full back Paul Wellens who really impressed with his faultless defence complemented by some energetic support play. Whenever there was half a break by the big men in the middle the Saints number one was up there to carry on the movement.

It was a sweet and sour occasion in some respects – although the young Saints in particular emerged with credit, it was at the cost of losing skipper Paul Sculthorpe with knee ligament damage after only 18 minutes.

The occasion was another feather in the cap of the Saints class of 2006. However, it meant Daniel Anderson and his backroom staff had had an awkward week preparing for the trip to Wakefield, with Saints having 10 players on Tuesday international duty – the eight Great Britain lads plus Kiwis Willie Talau and Vinnie Anderson.

But there was no bleating, rather there was a determination that the slightly scratchy bounce back win against Salford was consolidated with another one at Belle Vue.

"Morale is very important and confidence can leave pretty quickly and self-doubt can creep in. It only takes a good win to rediscover that confidence and momentum. We need to back up our performance at Wakefield on Sunday and start to get on a run again," said Anderson.

13

Paul Wellens – the Rock of St Helens

The Saints class of 2006 was pulled in from across the world – the big overseas contingent flew in from Australia, Samoa and New Zealand, and domestically players from Dewsbury, Castleford, Wakefield, Hull, Wigan, Barrow, Bradford and Oldham were added to the mix.

But for all the globetrotting and cheque writing Saints' chairman Eamonn McManus had done in constructing that squad it was two of the born and bred St Heleners who provided the big, beating heart of the team.

Powerhouse number nine Keiron Cunningham was the driving force in the middle, but at the back, marshalling the defence, Paul Wellens was untouchable. In a team jam-packed with stars and big personalities, it has to be a special effort to catch the eye of those people picking the awards. And consummate professional Wellens did just that, with his meticulous preparation for each and every game yielding a consistently high quality performance.

In the words of Daniel Anderson, "Wello slaughtered the awards." He walked away with Man of Steel, Player's Player of the Year, the Harry Sunderland Award, Saints Player of the Year and was listed in the Super League Dream team.

Reflecting on those individual and team achievements some seven years later Wellens understandably recalls the 2006 with particular fondness. He said: "I was consistent – I was playing very well and that season I played well all year. I very rarely heard 'Wello did not play that well today'. If I did not play well I just had a good game, not a very good game. I was confident, I was scoring tries, making them and stopping them.

"There was a tackle there at Odsal when we lost to Bradford where I bundled Lesley Vainikolo over the sidelines. Nobody did that with 'The Volcano' back then. But at that time I was fit, strong and confident and was in a really good place. A lot of that was because I was just focusing on Paul Wellens because everything else was taken care of.

"It was no surprise that I picked up all those individual awards that year because I was playing in one of the most well-oiled units that Super League had ever seen and it was such a joy to play for.

"I spent no time worrying about what other people were doing. I knew the wings had their bit covered, likewise the halves. Longy and Keiron are looking after the leadership roles. It was a carefree night out, like playing in the park with my mates as a kid – it was that simple for me.

"And Daniel every now and then would grab me and give me a little pointer here and there. He very rarely did a lot of work with me, he would advise me to look at some points of my game but it was never overkill. I just knew where I needed to be in the team."

Wellens scored 22 tries from 33 appearances that season, crediting the arrival of Leon Pryce at stand off as a major contributor to that fact.

He said: "Most of my tries that year came through support play. I'd like to know how many I got off the back of Leon's big rangy stride getting through the line and coming up with the offload.

"Leon came to us that year and took a little bit of getting used to but once I did we worked really well together because I just had to follow him. If he got his arms free there would be opportunities for me – or later on if I could back up the person he had released on the inside. Leon was crucial in making space for other players."

Like every other member of the previous year's roster, 2005 had burned into him, and had been a big motivating factor leading into that grand slam winning-season. There was real belief in defeat, something that had been missing when the team had limped out of play-off campaigns in 2001, 2003 and 2004.

Wellens added: "On the balance of form we were by far the best team in the competition in 2005, but the semi-final defeat by Hull in the Challenge Cup and the home losses to Leeds and Bradford in the play-offs were really frustrating.

"Hull was probably the most disappointing one because we simply did not perform well and were absolutely dominated. The other two we look at differently because we were busted through injuries, having lost Sean Long in that game at Wigan a couple of weeks previously, which meant we had Scott Moore in the halves and he was only a young kid at the time.

"The way we fought and the effort we showed in those two games was great and that gave us a lot of confidence going into 2006. We knew that once we got things right the actual attitude was all there and we just needed to fine-tune one or two areas."

There was a marked difference between the team of 2005 – the one that had to settle for the League Leaders' Shield – and the one that followed it. Wellens has his own viewpoint.

"The difference between the two years for me personally was a sense of determination but also a confidence that nearly bordered on arrogance in a way. We knew we were very good. We only had to look around the dressing room at the people sat around – and look at the people who could not get in the team, good men like Nick Fozzard and Vinnie Anderson, and that gave an indication of how good we were.

"You looked about the dressing room and see Jamie Lyon – confident player, Longy, Leon, Keiron, myself at the time – all really confident players in key positions and all playing well.

"In terms of the salary cap we had two young kids who came in – James Graham and James Roby – who were probably on relatively little money at the time. They came in and performed like internationals. It shouldn't happen, but it did.

"So in a lot respects we were really lucky like that yet there was a real focus with the group and Daniel focused a fair bit of accountability and discipline in the group.

"We only lost four games, but we never lost a match by more than four points, which shows that we were more than competitive in every game. The one we lost by four was the young lads in Catalan when we took a weakened team. Our youngsters went over there and nearly pulled off a scalp against a pretty experienced Catalan side."

There are a couple of myths that subsequently did the rounds in the years after that season – often by those fans who struggled to come to terms with the five subsequent Grand Final losses and the style of rugby that the team played under Mick Potter. For some of those fans, there was a longing desire to turn the clock back to the flashiness of the Millward era and some of the Anderson period gets air-brushed in the rewriting of history. That first myth was Saints compromised their attacking prowess to add steel to the defence, but the tries scored by the outside backs in the Super League points total of 939 tells its own story.

The other was that because both finalists Saints faced that year – Hull and Huddersfield – were not members of the big four club, it meant that they had 'nowt to beat'. Wellens poured a bucket of cold water over both of them.

"It really is a myth that our attack suffered – our points scored was up there with the most successful teams we have ever had.

"As for there being nothing to beat – when we beat Leeds towards the end of the year at Knowsley Road – they were a team full of big names. Jamie Peacock, Kevin Sinfield, Keith Senior, Gareth Ellis, Danny McGuire, Rob Burrow Clinton Toopi – Leeds had internationals all over the field.

"Hull were up there with some of the best Super League sides we have played – they had shown that the year previously when they beat Leeds to win the Challenge Cup.

"Also, Peter Sharp had done an unbelievable job at Hull. They were a really strong team. It became no surprise to us that they became our main rivals and given the cup win the year before we expected them to be up there."

Saints were the only team with 100 per cent after three games and after round two on 17 February they leapt to the top of the table and were front runners all the way through to October. Under the top six, before the dreadful top eight was introduced, there was still a big advantage in finishing top of the pile. There was also a sense of pride and attitude to keep going from the off.

The full back continued: "Our first game was away to Harlequins at the Stoop and that gave an indication of how well we had started. That is always a difficult place to start because they had some good players there at the time. We had a tough early part but then ended up running away with the game that gave us a lot of confidence to go from there.

"That said I was always – not pessimistic – but sort of 'let's not get carried away'. I did not want to lose focus and think we were too good. In the last home game of the regular season we battered Leeds 54-18 at home; it was the game in which Paul Anderson kicked the goal off the touchline. We were 30 odd points up at half-time, Jamie Lyon had scored a hat-trick and I just remember coming off at half-time thinking 'God, we are this good'. Leeds were a good team and yet we tore them to shreds. That was a point in my career where I got past the point of confidence and thought we are nearly unbeatable if we get it right."

Comparisons with that Saints team of 2006 can be made to those full time Wigan teams in the 1988-95 – the pre salary cap and level playing field teams that won eight Challenge Cups in a row. No team had been as dominant and as expected, nay, guaranteed to win as this. And it was not as if Saints had used extra spending power above what their rivals were lashing out. Wellens believes good fortune favoured them in their recruitment.

"What we did as a club was get lucky. We signed Paul Anderson who everyone thought 'what are we signing him for, he's hardly playing for Bradford?' and yet he was phenomenal for two years.

"Saints used him in the right way and got great value from him. Robes and James Graham who were probably on a pittance at the time, performed like seasoned internationals. We shifted Leon to six and he became the best stand off in the competition. It seemed that every bit of business we did at the time came to fruition. We got lucky in that respect."

With everything being directed by Sean Long at scrum half, that left Leon Pryce to play a much freer role at six, something the laid-back, lanky Bradfordian revelled in.

"All the play came through Longy – that is why Leon loved it so much. If you absolve Leon of all organisational responsibility and say 'play to the best of your ability' he would lap it up. You still need structure but what he had inside him was Keiron and Longy who would get us where we needed to be.

"Leon could go where he wanted and when he wanted and I would do the same off the back of his play. Leon did call some shots, he and Longy worked very well together, but Leon would call plays off the back of a structure that Keiron and Longy had organised.

"They would basically say, 'this is where we are going, this is what we are doing'. We were getting to the point where we were having plays off the back of plays, off the back of plays. So Keiron would call something, Longy would do something off the back of that and then Leon would interject off that. Jamie Lyon and myself would chime in on the back of that. We had so many different options that it was just a case of let's go," Wellens said.

Pryce, however, was not simply a Rolls Royce player to be driven out on special occasions. He ended up doing his fair share of defence – but it was not a bed of roses all the time. And Wellens revealed one occasion where he earned the wrath of coach Daniel Anderson – and in doing so sent a message to the rest of the team.

"Leon was always thought of as a great attacking player who did not really fancy the defensive side of things. But Leon, particularly in that year, was fantastic in defence. On the left side with Lee Gilmour, Willie Talau and Jon Wilkin they got a really good defensive unit going. Leon's whole mentality changed under Daniel which gave an indication of what he expected of his players.

"An indication of that approach to defence came in one of the games we lost – 20-18 at Bradford. Leon is better at telling the tale, but on this occasion he was not getting off his line quick enough. Daniel came in at half-time and it was one of the Alex Ferguson 'hair dryer' moments and it was basically square on Leon. 'You get off your line, not in the eighth minute, not in the fifth minute, in the first minute,' he barked.

"He tore shreds off him and it was probably the first time in Leon's career that anyone had really berated him and from then on it changed Leon's mentality. You could see him thinking 'wow, I am in a different environment here'. Certainly different than the one he was in at Bradford, where he was the local lad sitting comfortably. It was a defining moment in the season because although it was Leon who was getting the telling off, the message was for everybody," Wellens said.

It was the team of all talents – but the balance was there too, with grafters complementing those with the silky skills. Wellens was keen to sing the praises of two of the club's often unsung heroes.

"In that season a lot of people will talk about myself, because I obviously got some accolades, Jamie, Longy and Keiron – but the two most important people for me were Jason Hooper and Mike Bennett because they were at the coal face.

"While everyone else was picking up awards, they were grafting – I don't think Mike missed a tackle all season. He missed a big chunk of the season, but when he came back he played every week and did not miss and that gives you an indication of what the coaching staff thought of Mike Bennett.

"I speak to a lot of juniors at the club now and everybody looks at us and says 'I want to be Jamie Lyon, I want to do the flick pass, I want to be Sean Long, Keiron Cunningham, this or that.' I say 'try and be Mike Bennett' because ability will only take you so far. It is your attitude, commitment, work ethic and willingness to work. Ability wise – and he will tell you himself – Mike should probably have not got in that team. But he got in on attitude, commitment and work ethic. That is my message to kids – get that one right and the ability will take care of the rest. You give yourself a fair chance that way."

After missing the Challenge Cup run and a large part of the season with injury Bennett came in just in time to make a pitch for the Grand Final, and although he leapt above Vinnie Anderson for that third forward on the bench spot, he essentially replaced the injured Paul Sculthorpe at the back end of the season.

A two-times Man of Steel, Sculthorpe had been a giant during Saints' glory years since signing from Warrington in 1998. Tough, skilful and the ultimate competitor, Sculthorpe should have been guaranteed a spot – but he was never 100 per cent in 2006. Even when he battled to get himself passed fit to play he was never the same player. And that did leave Saints and coach Daniel Anderson with a problem.

Wellens explained how the potentially unsettling and difficult situation had to be handled. He said: "Scully was a huge and influential part of the team, but he was in the team and out the team for long periods. What we had to do and what Daniel did was to play a way without Scully. If he was there, then great, but if he wasn't we had a mindset that it didn't matter.

"That is how we had to channel it. I saw it at first hand – Scully trying so hard – working his backside off in the gym to get fit. It was heartbreaking to see him keep breaking down. But for the good of the team we had to channel our thoughts into what we needed to do to be successful. We could not wait to see if Scully was coming back. Time waits for no man."

There were other players missing out, especially for the big games, with internationals Vinnie Anderson and Nick Fozzard playing 27 and 23 games respectively that year, but being overlooked for the showpieces at Twickenham and Old Trafford.

"Both Nick and Vinnie missed out on the big games and were obviously disappointed but what I will say is that although they were disappointed they never shook the applecart. They accepted the decision and supported the boys. I am sure they were disappointed with the coach's decision but it was never visible. They still came out and trained hard and supported the boys 100 per cent. That is important again.

"If you are in a team and get given disappointing news and you then walk around the training field sulking, it can rub off on the rest of the group. But those two always put the team first which was pretty important," Wellens said.

When Wellens speaks the passion for his home town club – his only pro team – oozes out of every pore. It is in his family, in his blood – if he was a stick of Blackpool rock he would have a red vee and a stickman running right through the middle of him. It is easy to see why coach Daniel Anderson described him as, along with Keiron Cunningham, the heartbeat of the team. Loving the club and its history just comes so naturally to him – as it does to any young kid who spent their formative years cheering from the Popular Side. As such he respects the traditions that run through the club, particularly the reverence and esteem that some of the legends are held. And fittingly one of those legends from the last team to win all available cups was there to present the jerseys ahead of the Challenge Cup Final at Twickenham.

Wellens explained the effect on the team of meeting a slender, frail old man with an Afrikaner brogue – one of the town's most illustrious adopted sons.

He said: "Tom van Vollenhoven came to the hotel and spoke to us the night before the final. Obviously, none of us had seen him play but he was a legend of the club and when he spoke even overseas guys were made aware of that and respected it. There was a real 'buy-in' from the overseas players of the culture of the club and it is something now I try to encourage. It is not enough to just come and play for the team. I play for St Helens but I think it is important to understand what it stands for, who has played here and why they played here and what they got from those experiences.

"That is what we constantly need to be driving – even though we have moved stadiums now. What was Knowsley Road? What did it mean? That is something we should always embrace – every single one of those players whether from St Helens or not understood it. Even though Leon had been at Bradford for 10 years and was Bulls through and through, he understood and bought into it and that is really important.

"2006 was something else and the fact that this book is about that year spells out how good a year it was. At that time there is a tendency of supporters and players to think that the good times, success and trophies is going to automatically continue, but this is sport; rugby, football and cricket teams go through phases and transitions. The last five or six years have been extremely really tough because of what we have come from in terms of all the great players that we have had.

"What we need to do is embrace that and remember it, but accept that we can be a great side again but it will be on totally different terms with different players playing a different way. That is what we have got to strive to do again.

"We have to use 2006 as a benchmark to strive to get back there."

14

July

The effects of the baking heat and fatigue from the gruelling schedule led to an old school scoreboard blow-out at Belle Vue with Saints easing off in the second half and very nearly getting dragged back into a game. They saw off Wakefield 52-36 – the first time they had broken the half-century barrier in a Super League game in 2006. However the down side of that was a leaky defensive performance littered with missed tackles which produced a basketball type scoreline and meant the match was in the balance until late in the game.

Saints had good reason for a slightly off-colour performance. Not only did they take the field with seven of the players who had backed up from a midweek Test, they lost two of those through injury early on in the match.

Packman Lee Gilmour was knocked out making a tackle on Semi Tadulala in the second minute and played no further part in the game.

Saints lost Willie Talau in the second half, leading to further reorganisation out wide and limiting coach Daniel Anderson's substitution options on a day that they were probably needed most due to the sky high temperatures. Jason Hooper gave his usual gutsy performance, being well supported by Jason Cayless and big Paul Anderson. James Roby returned to the first team with a sparkling performance after a spell in the Academy and Jon Wilkin, too, showed some classy touches. The partisan and frequently hostile Belle Vue has never been the happiest of hunting grounds for Saints, and when Trinity moved eight points clear fears mounted that it was going to be one of those days. But five unanswered tries gave Saints a 40-18 lead and although they eased off Saints still had enough juice to claim the victory.

With Leeds and Hull continuing to pile on the wins, there was no room for a Saints slip-up at the summit.

Anderson said: "We are pretty banged up at the moment and are mentally and physically tired. We are just hanging tough at the moment because we cannot see the end of the competition. We have to match our opposition for enthusiasm and attitude. I think we have more skilful players in our team, but if we don't turn up with the right attitude we will get turned over.

"We have as bad an injury situation as anyone else, but we have Keiron Cunningham, Sean Long and Paul Wellens really doing a great job for us in keeping the team nice and tight."

Off the field Saints' board was tasked with filling the most illustrious boots in Super League with the not unsurprising news that Jamie Lyon was returning Down Under at the end of the season. The 2005 Man of Steel Lyon had signed a four-year deal with NRL giants Manly – but he made sure he was going to do right by the club that had restored his appetite for rugby league before he even contemplated packing his suitcases.

Coach Daniel Anderson said: "Obviously it is disappointing news for the club, but it was not totally unexpected for those of us who train every day with him. If Jamie Lyon was on his own then I think he would be staying, but he has a partner and a son to consider."

Turning towards the dry track that Saints were now playing on – which was bringing out the best in the Australian speedster – Anderson added: "Jamie is the classic dry weather footballer, who has really come into his own the last couple of weeks with the weather drying out. We laughed in round one this year when he intercepted on the halfway line but was almost caught by a front rower at Harlequins, but nobody looks like catching him now. When he gets the ball in the clear, he just goes.

"He is having a huge impact all over the field in attack and defence. Just look at the number of tries he has created for Ade Gardner. He has been fantastic this last couple of weeks for us with some things we haven't seen for a while – such as long distance tries. His change of direction has been exceptional as has been his try-scoring sniff. He is in a rich vein of form and we should enjoy it while he is here."

So Saints were having no trouble crossing the opposition whitewash and despite having one row of the main stand packed with Test players, Saints still had enough quality on the park to clock up a second successive half century, seeing off the stubborn French resistance to beat Catalan 52-26.

With Willie Talau and Lee Gilmour joining longer-term casualties Francis Meli and Paul Sculthorpe on the sidelines, Saints shuffled their line-up and gave a debut to 17-year-old Ste Tyrer who played the full second half on the wing. By that stage the two points required to keep Saints on top of the Super League pile were already in the bag, with the leaders coming from behind to slay the Dragons with six tries in a 25-minute blitzkrieg.

Among them was Sean Long, who showed great footwork and determination to score his 100th Super League touchdown. James Roby was rewarded with his first try of the season – becoming the last regular squad player to break his duck – and his magnificent break also sent big Paul Anderson powering over for a try.

The Saints boss explained how difficult it was for the club with a twin track focus, with the Challenge Cup semi-final getting closer and closer.

"It is still a tough patch for us – an interesting part of the year because we have two competitions to focus on. It is difficult because Hull and Leeds keep on winning, which keeps us under the pump in the league. But I have to keep an eye on Hull KR in a few weeks to make sure we are flying in that one. We cannot go into a cup semi-final half-cocked or under strength," he said.

Given the way they had started, and how much emphasis Daniel Anderson had placed on fitting his blueprint on the club since his arrival, Saints' defence had been surprisingly leaky in July.

As ever Anderson had an understanding and explanation for the apparent drop-off – and an ambition and aspiration on that score.

"We cannot be mentally and physically focused for 35 weeks of the season, and it is inevitable that we are going to have patches of indifferent form. We will defend a lot better at the back end of the year, but it is difficult to maintain the intensity in defence for the whole season. If we can finish the season with the best defensive record then that will be a feather in our cap.

"If Leeds and Hull were not so hard on our heels we could maybe relax a little. But we can't and therefore have to push the players to train hard to keep their bodies really toned and wired up. Then they have to play. Every competition point is important at the moment – and that is shown by each game we play," he said.

Saints' 30-24 victory over Harlequins – combined with Leeds' loss – opened up a four-point lead at the Super League summit, but it was a very jittery display characterised by a succession of handling errors, that brought sighs of frustration from some among the lowest league crowd of the season – a relatively meagre 7,950.

There was mitigation – with Saints' roll call of injuries meaning they opted to play a conservative, close to the ruck, up the middle brand of football that is probably not welcomed by fans who like to see a bit more flair.

With Sean Long out with a leg injury, teenager Matty Smith was drafted in for only his second senior start and despite scoring his first try, he had something of a mixed game. Saints were never able to coast, and it took a last quarter try from wing Ade Gardner from a suspiciously forward looking basketball type pass from Jamie Lyon to clinch it.

Throughout July Saints had won despite conceding totals of 36, 26 and 24 points – unthinkable at the start of the year. With a trip to Headingley next up Anderson knew that conceding so many points against their nearest rivals on the ladder would not deliver the goods. It was going to be a tough game, especially with both clubs in semi-final action the following week and made even trickier by Leeds losing to Castleford the weekend before.

"Leeds are packed with internationals, well coached and will be smarting from that loss and that represents a great challenge for us. Cas did us a big favour, but you have to be aware of a wounded team.

"If we win we have a six point lead, if we lose we are back in the mire fighting for a top three spot. If you have a look at the rest of the season, there is a chance that we could play Leeds five more times this year, so in poker terms it is not an 'all in' game.

"As much as I want us to open up a six-point gap, I won't risk players who could injure themselves. I cannot see Leeds doing that either," Anderson said.

As it was Saints had another obstacle to clear, overcoming the 68th minute dismissal of ace Aussie centre Jamie Lyon to down Leeds 18-14 on their own midden and move six points clear at the Super League summit. The gutsy victory, Saints' first at Headingley since 2002, was built on a solid team effort with youngsters James Graham and James Roby really earning their spurs. There were also outstanding performances from try scorers Lee Gilmour and Maurie Fa'asavalu, with the versatile Jon Wilkin earning plenty of plaudits for the way he adapted to the half back role in the absence of late withdrawal Sean Long.

Typically, given the country had been sweltering in a heatwave all week, the game was played in a torrential downpour, which started bang on kick off and ended in Leeds about an hour after the game. But those 2,000 travelling fans, who were left with no option but to stand in the open terrace, did not flinch an inch. And they were singing in the rain at the end of an enthralling 80 minutes.

The tackling on both sides was as explosively ferocious, with Gareth Ellis's massive hit on Jason Cayless setting the tone for a thunderous encounter.

Ellis opened the scoring for Leeds, but that was cancelled out by one from interchange prop Fa'asavalu, who bashed his way over the line. In 2006 no other player was breaking the first tackle as cleanly and as consistently as the blockbusting former Samoan rugby union World Cup flanker and that night Fa'asavalu's raw power caused consternation in the Leeds ranks every time he took the ball up.

The crowd lapped it up with cries of "Maurie, Maurie, Maurie!" ringing out.

Keith Senior's 80-metre interception try and Sinfield's conversion and penalty gave Leeds a 14-6 lead after tough-as-teak centre

Willie Talau traded punches with Chev Walker and both were sin binned. But Saints kept their heads up and on the stroke of half-time Wellens slipped a fine pass to Gilmour, who took advantage of the soggy Headingley turf to slide over in a single movement. Lyon's touchline goal cut the deficit to 14-12 as the hooter sounded.

Although the second half yielded only one score, that did nothing to diminish what was an enthralling spectacle for the 17,700 sell-out crowd. Roby, who had replaced Keiron Cunningham just before the break, remained on the field and operated at half back when the Saints stand-in skipper returned to the fold.

And the nippy youngster caused endless problems for the Rhinos with his usual bursts from acting half back complemented by a greater degree of handling and kicking. Leeds did have a much more accomplished kicking game – with the boot of Kevin Sinfield giving Saints a thorough examination. However, it was a test that Wellens in particular passed with flying colours.

With the visitors' line holding firm, Saints took their chance on 64 minutes when Cunningham's tormenting diagonal run from dummy half produced paralysis in the Leeds defence before delivering a flat pass to send Gilmour powering through.

Lyon goaled, but was given his marching orders four minutes later when he followed through on Rob Burrow after the kick. The sight of the diminutive scrum half hitting the deck and with the noise of baying South Stand hollering its disapproval gave referee Ashley Klein all the encouragement he needed to go straight for his pocket and produce the red card.

Despite being a man down, Saints held on to complete a double and after the drift of the previous three games it was reassuring to see that steel was still there when needed. Anderson saw other pleasing facets to the performance which showed that they had indeed moved on from the previous year when the absence of two key men – most notably Sean Long – saw them ultimately come unstuck when it mattered.

"Much has been made of the fact that we won a close encounter against Leeds without Longy and Scully. That is something we had trouble doing at the back end of last year, when we relied on

Keiron Cunningham and Jamie Lyon for almost everything.

"Although Keiron remains as difficult to contain, we have so many other players who are now willing to take on added responsibility.

"On top of that Paul Wellens' form is absolutely outstanding, and that has not gone unnoticed. We have tried to tweak some of his attacking play and use some of his strengths differently to last season. He is very easy to coach and very communicative to the coaching staff and I believe he continues to improve every week."

It was just the tonic Saints needed heading into the semi-final clash against giant-killers Hull KR, who had surprisingly toppled Warrington in the quarter finals.

And they received a further double boost with scrum half Sean Long recovering from the leg injury that had forced him to miss the previous two games and Jamie Lyon being cleared to play after the RFL Disciplinary Committee deemed that sending off was sufficient punishment for his late tackle at Leeds.

Prior to the hearing, coach Anderson said: "Jamie will carry the fairly substantial stigma of being sent off for the rest of his career.

"He is a genuinely honest and clean player and that challenge was just a dumb play and out of character."

Saints were revisiting the Huddersfield ground that has been their Challenge Cup semi-final graveyard on their previous two visits in 2003 and 2005. After slumping to something of a shock the previous year against eventual winners Hull FC, nobody at Knowsley Road was taking anything for granted this time against their Humberside neighbours despite it looking like a men against boys contest.

Anderson saw a chance of redemption that had been a long time coming.

"When we lost to Hull and Bradford in June we had seven days to redeem ourselves. But if you look at our loss to Hull in last year's semi-final we have had 12 months to wait, but now we have a chance to redeem ourselves. It is in our own hands," he said.

However, no stone was left unturned in preparing – and to use Anderson's much used phrase "due diligence" was observed in the build up.

"I never underestimate teams and we are preparing diligently for this one. Hull KR have high aspirations and plenty of players with Super League potential and Justin Morgan is a good coach."

It was never in doubt as ruthless Saints booked their fourth Challenge Cup Final spot in six years with a clinical 50-0 win over the National League One outfit.

If the difference in size between the sides was noticeable in the warm-up, it became even more evident in the heat of the battle. And, while the half-century and nine tries scored by Saints told one part of the story, the nil points conceded explained why it was never going to be a day for the underdogs.

Saints' defensive line was up early to meet Rovers head-on, and snuff out the slightest flicker of them being able to launch a promising attacking move. The sight of Francis Meli flying off his wing to smash Rovers' chunky loose forward Tommy Gallagher in the sixth minute underlined Saints' defensive tenacity. And it was relentless for the full 80 minutes, with no hint of guards being dropped and consolation points being conceded.

Fittingly, Paul Wellens put the icing on the cake when he threaded his way through a dispirited Rovers defence to bring up both Saints' 50 and his own personal milestone of 100 tries for the club. After spending three games on the nervous 99 mark, the in-form full back showed real pride in his achievement as he celebrated with jubilant fans.

Wellens said: "It felt fantastic to reach the century mark. When you start out your career for St Helens I don't think you ever envisage scoring 100 tries for the club. To reach the mark in a cup semi-final meant an awful lot to me. I had been stuck on 99 for about three weeks and a lot of my family and friends had been talking about it for a while so it was great to get that try."

Wellens said the squad also took satisfaction from the resounding win that saw them nil The Robins adding: "Everyone expected us to win so it was important we came up with a good performance as well. It would not have been satisfactory just to have got through to the final."

Anderson was equally delighted having put right a few wrongs from 2005, explaining: "There was a steel in our determination and focus before the game. It was quite ironic that we were in the same dressing room at the Galpharm Stadium as we were last year when we were beaten by Hull. And, in a way, that disappointment was something that a number of the players and myself drew on in the hour leading up to the game. We spoke about how it was in our own hands to redeem ourselves and we did that.

"Hull KR are a very good team but they simply caught us on a day when we were absolutely fantastic. To be fair, from Monday last week I didn't believe we would lose that game because of our preparation – you could almost smell the players' focus."

15

Saints' Awesome Foursome

The history of sport has been illuminated by some legendary teams over the years. There have been plenty of dazzling XIs, XIIIs and XVs that have really stood out over the decades – the 1970 World Cup winning Brazilian footballers, the 1982 Invincible Kangaroos and the great Welsh outfit of the 70s and the All Blacks class of 1987. Flair in abundance but balanced by a layer of people prepared to do the heavy lifting, not all of it always automatically recognised. It is always a matter for debate no matter the shape or size of the ball – what really made those outstanding, invincible and entertaining sporting teams so dominant and so iconic?

The awe-inspiring West Indies team from the mid 70s to mid 80s, which made many a pre-Super League summer interesting, had a plethora of star men. For all that exemplary batting from Gordon Greenidge, those swashbuckling strokes from Viv Richards and great leadership from Lancashire's adopted son Clive Lloyd – one thing made those teams stand out – the fast bowlers. The four blokes who worked in tandem to send the cork and leather ball hurtling down the wicket laid the platform of that utterly devastating team from the Caribbean. Whether it was the one that made Brian Close wince and Tony Greig eat his "grovel" words in 1976 or those that took out the first two cricket World Cups in 1975 and 1979, it was that relentless pace attack that was the key to victory. When Michael Holding and Joel Garner had finished with their shift, on came Andy Roberts and Colin Croft. There was no respite from the 90 mph punishment from the Four Horsemen.

And just like the 70s and early 80s batsmen got sick of the sight of that Windies whirlwind and the punishment they were about to inflict; there was probably a similar feeling across the pitches of the M62 corridor in 2006. The rugby league equivalent was seeing Saints' front row steaming in, a props union comprising four from Paul Anderson, Jason Cayless, Maurie Fa'asavalu, James Graham and Nick Fozzard. Although each one had a distinctive style, it was the relentless size and power that defences had to cope with. There was never any respite and after the opposing men in the trenches had finally seen the back of Anderson and Cayless, over the hill would come young buck Graham and the explosive Samoan Fa'asavalu. And although he missed out on the big games, the streetwise big and bony bruiser Fozzard also played a big part in laying a winning platform in games that year, contributing to 23 of the matches that term.

With go-forward generated on an industrial scale, at their heels the twin force of Keiron Cunningham and James Roby had a beano at dummy half, and the rest of it – from the halves out to the flanks – revelled in the space the big men had earned.

It was a front row that had been put together methodically by coach Daniel Anderson. Although he had inherited Fozzard, Anderson, Graham and Fa'asavalu the latter two were really given their head after the new boss took the reins. And once Anderson had got his feet under the table in the middle of 2005 he began to seek out that often under-rated but most crucial of ingredients – the starting prop. Jason Cayless was a top drawer, hard-nosed but skilful front rower in his prime when he was lured from the bright lights Sydney Roosters and the NRL. In swapping Bondi Beach for the Burgy banks he added the X factor to the red vee front row ranks.

There were departures, with speedy but lightweight prop Mark Edmondson allowed to go Down Under, ironically to Cayless' old Roosters club. Alas the likeable lad was plagued with a shoulder injury, managing only two games with the Roosters and then being similarly hampered when he returned to Blighty with Salford. And Keith Mason, who had answered Saints' front row crisis back in the middle of 2003 when he returned to England from Melbourne, was surplus to requirements as a result of the rapid advancement of Fa'asavalu and Graham. He was despatched to newly promoted

Jamie Lyon brushes off Karl Temata on his way to an opening
day try against Harlequins

Jamie Lyon and Nick Fozzard chase a kick to the try line
against Bradford. Both miss!

Sean Long faces up to Bradford's hooker Terry Newton for the first time since the previous September's incident which left the Saints scrum half with a fractured cheekbone

Nuts and bolts man Jason Hooper shows his handing skills against Wigan in the Good Friday game. He scored twice that day in a comfortable 48-10 victory

Lee Gilmour brushes off the challenge of then Wigan and now England rugby union wingman Chris Ashton

Vinnie Anderson knocks the wind out of Wigan second row man Danny Tickle's sails after a monster tackle which became a YouTube sensation

The front row union of Jason Cayless and Maurie Fa'asavalu combines to terrorise the Catalan Dragons defence in the Challenge Cup quarter final

Seven of the eight-strong Saints contingent who played for Great Britain in the one-off test against New Zealand at Knowsley Road. Leon Pryce, Paul Wellens, Keiron Cunningham, Sean Long, Lee Gilmour, James Graham and Ade Gardner celebrate, with Paul Sculthorpe being an early casualty of the game

Jamie Lyon is shown the red card for his challenge on Leeds' Rob Burrow

Hull KR face the destructive effect of a Francis Meli tackle in the Challenge Cup semi final

Willie Talau touches down in the Challenge Cup semi final hammering of Hull KR

Paul Wellens shows his elation after Saints qualified for the Challenge Cup Final

Saints' 'Yorkshire Bus' comprising Leon Pryce, Paul Anderson, Lee Gilmour and Nick Fozzard celebrate the Challenge Cup semi final win

Prop James Graham gets measured up for his Challenge Cup Final outfit

The legendary Tom van Vollenhoven hands Keiron Cunningham (top) and Jason Hooper (bottom) their Challenge Cup Final jerseys on the eve of the match at Twickenham

Sean Long scampers in for a
try against Huddersfield in the
Challenge Cup Final

Maurie Fa'asavalu charges
up the middle as James Roby
races up in support during
the Challenge Cup Final

Jon Wilkin celebrates his second try
at Twickenham along with James
Graham and Paul Wellens

Jamie Lyon zips in at the
corner in the Cup Final win
over Huddersfield

Paul Sculthorpe and Keiron Cunningham take a handle each to
lift the Challenge Cup

Maurie Fa'asavalu leads the post match celebrations in the Twickenham
dressing rooms after the Challenge Cup Final win over Huddersfield

A long soak of success. Leon Pryce, Maurie Fa'asavalu, Lee Gilmour, Jason Hooper and Paul Wellens in the post match Twickenham baths

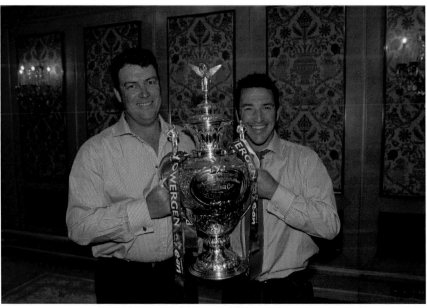

Saints coach Daniel Anderson and technical adviser Alan Wilson celebrate the Challenge Cup win over Huddersfield

Second rower Mike Bennett in the
thick of the action against Leeds

James Graham and Jason Hooper
close in on Leeds' Rob Burrow

The team and coaching staff celebrate winning the League Leaders
Shield after the win over Leeds

Saints second row man Jon Wilkin reaches over for one of his 11 tries scored in 2006 – this one against Warrington in September.

Wing Ade Gardner scoring one of his 31 tries – again against Warrington in September

Paul Wellens also adds his name to the scoresheet against the Wolves as he dives over for one of his 22 tries scored in that season

Even the Saints Academy team got in on the act, beating Wigan in the Grand Final at Knowsley Road

Acclimatisation! Leon Pryce, Jamie Lyon, Willie Talau, Jason Hooper and Sean Long get used to the Old Trafford changing rooms

Daniel Anderson leads the teams out amid the noise and
fireworks at Old Trafford

Jamie Lyon dashes through the
Hull defence in the Grand Final
at Old Trafford

Stand off Leon Pryce strides
through for the crucial try
just before half time in the
Grand Final at Old Trafford

Sean Long raises the Super League trophy to complete the clean sweep

James Roby, James Graham, Ade Gardner, Mike Bennett and Apollo Perelini celebrate winning the league

This is what we came for! Saints chairman Eamonn McManus looks as proud as punch as he holds the Super League trophy with coach Daniel Anderson at Old Trafford

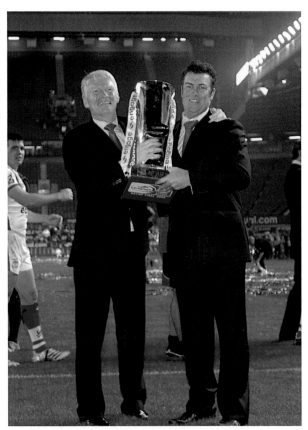

The morning after the night before – the homecoming Saints show off their haul of trophies

Ade Gardner leaps to take Sean Long's cross kick to touch down against Brisbane Broncos in the 2007 World Club Challenge at the Reebok

Paul Sculthorpe came off the bench to dive over for a crucial try against Brisbane in the World Club Challenge

Job done! Sean Long raises the World Club Challenge trophy at the Reebok after beating Brisbane to complete the silverware haul of all four trophies

All photographs courtesy of Bernard Platt

Castleford on loan for his last remaining year of his contract. Saints may not have wanted Mason's services any more, but when Millward – by then at Wigan – came in to try and take him from Castleford, chairman Eamonn McManus understandably put the blockers on it. He was, after all, still a Saints player. There was plenty of bad blood between the clubs, particularly given that for a few weeks during Millward's brief honeymoon at the JJB in May 2005 the press had speculated about how many Saints stars would follow their old boss to Wigan. As it happened only hooker Mickey Higham had gone after being warehoused by Bradford before swapping places with Terry Newton.

Although Saints props had different styles and roles, and they complemented each other, size mattered. Midway through the season Daniel Anderson paid tribute to the variety of qualities offered by his props.

"There is a subtle difference between them all – you can stuff the big fella Paul Anderson in the middle and he will suck in three blokes. And Nick Fozzard is a big bloke who performs a similar role.

'Then we have Jason Cayless who has got tremendous foot speed for a front rower and Maurie Fa'asavalu is probably the only front rower in the competition who consistently makes clean breaks and run away, then we have James Graham who has been in fantastic form.

"I can't work out who is the best but they certainly lay a platform for us in attack and defence," he said.

Anderson was the veteran, being 33 when he signed from the Bradford Bulls club that he served with some distinction between 1997 and 2004. It was a signing greeted with some bemusement initially – indeed one exasperated past player expressed the off the record view that he had heard: "Anderson's legs have gone, he's past it." Other fans, no doubt fixated on another high-profile Aussie import to follow in the illustrious footsteps of David Fairleigh and Darren Britt, scratched their heads in a way they did when that other fine son of Castleford – Kevin Ward – was enticed across the Pennines for a Knowsley Road swansong. And once again those doubters gladly ate humble pie. They used to mine coal in Anderson and Ward's home town but the closures of Fryston in 1985, Glasshoughton in 1986 and Wheldale in 1987 has left Castleford without a working pit. Saints have nevertheless found a rich seam to mine in that time since, pulling out two veteran prop forwards who went on to be worth their considerable weight in coal. However, Anderson, unlike Ward who tragically badly broke a leg in his final game, was able to write a fairytale ending to his playing career – even slotting a touchline conversion in his last regular Super League game.

But Baloo's weighty contribution amounted to something far more significant than his one-off goalkicking party piece– it was his sheer physical presence, fearlessness and trusty hands that made him such a cornerstone of the pack. Whenever the opposition kicked off, finding Anderson for that big, safe first carry was usually high on the agenda.

Although the big man had won plenty with the Bulls – where he was also part of an awesome foursome comprising Stuart Fielden, Brian McDermott and Joe Vagana – that competitive streak and dissatisfaction with the way his first year in the red vee had panned out were big driving forces for the big man. Anderson was then, and is even more so now as a head coach, a straight talker not a politician or someone coveting a role in the diplomatic corps. He doesn't bother with tactical niceties of biting his tongue if someone asks what he views as a daft question – they are invariably told straight. That honesty was applied to his own performances and speaking at the height of Indian summer at Saints, just ahead of the semi-final clash against Hull KR, Baloo recalled the previous year's knockout by Hull FC and expressed his deep seated desire to erase that from memory.

The big man said: "For me personally last year's semi-final defeat has been a bit of a driving force for this season. It was embarrassing really – knowing how poorly I played personally and how we did as a team. But all credit to Hull they came and did a job on us, caught us on an off day and took the spoils."

Anderson was not alone in putting his hand up to a disappointing performance that day. But rather than getting down about it, he used it as motivation and it was clear that 12 months down the line Hull's then much poorer neighbours and rivals were going to cop the backlash.

He said: "It is totally out of the question that I will play again next year. I have come to terms with that and want to go out on a high. I had the chance to play on another year, but I did not simply want to take the money.

"I like to play every game to the best of my ability and if I had gone on and my form had started to dip I would not have wanted those who stand on the terraces to start saying 'look he's gone on a year too long. I am happy with my decision and hopefully I am going out on top."

In 2006 there was a common assumption that old head Anderson was an invaluable presence in teaching Fa'asavalu and Graham a few of his tricks, a few of the arts in the mastery of front row play. However, Anderson disagreed.

"I have probably learned as much off those two, just feeding off their sheer enthusiasm. I see that when I wrestle Maurie in training and he throws me all over the place. But if those players think they have got to challenge themselves to try and do this to me in training then it augurs well for the future," Anderson said.

At the time of the departure coach and namesake Daniel said: "He is as good as any front rower I have ever seen. The way he can hit the ball up if he wants to, he can pass the ball if he wants to. He is defensively outstanding for a big man – he is a brilliant front rower who will be a huge loss for us.

"He is a role model for front rowers and is fiery enough to make it as a coach. He gave me the death stare a number of times at the start of this year when I used to drag him off during the game. But we have worked out a rotation schedule that we use if we don't lose anyone through injury. You are always right when you are a player, but he will learn there is a little bit more in the world to deal with as a coach."

The Saints boss revealed that Anderson had been asked to stay on another year, but the player said his 'time was done'. "But I certainly didn't want him to play anywhere else if he was going to carry on."

Paul Wellens gave a good tactical insight on the way Anderson was deployed and the special tactics the team employed to get full value from the 19st unit.

Speaking some seven years after Baloo's departure at the end of the treble-winning campaign Wellens recalled: "Paul Anderson was the biggest, heaviest member of the squad. We used to have a rule of making sure we got three in the tackle to try and slow the ruck. We used to say to Baloo 'if there is ever two in the tackle, make sure you are three to lend your big, burly frame to the collision.'

"We'd also say that if he was in the tackle he stays at marker so the onus was on one of the other two to get back. What we did was conserve his (Anderson's) energy to get the best out of him. There was no point making a big bloke go back and forth in defence, play to his strengths. We did that and it worked because we ended up getting more minutes out of him."

Baloo was certainly contributing considerably more minutes than he was giving to the Bulls in his last few seasons there – something Apollo Perelini and Daniel Anderson took a great deal of professional satisfaction from.

They also took similar pride from the impact of Fa'asavalu who made rapid strides in the red vee in 2006. The explosive former Samoan World Cup flanker brought something else to the table, particularly when working off the back of what old heads Anderson and Cayless had already laid down. He had dynamism and a willingness to run through a brick wall and yet still make that ball available. Although he was not equipped to start the game that did not mean his impact status made him any way second rate. He, like fellow interchange prop Graham, was a vital part in the jigsaw.

Having watched it from close quarters, Apollo Perelini believes Fa'asavalu's selfless front row union associates did more than most to assist the strong running Samoan's development into a lethal, line-breaking ball carrier.

Perelini said: "Maurie had experienced front rowers around him, players who had been around a long time and been there and done it. Those players were willing to help him. That was the thing about our club – they were not afraid of losing their place to someone like Maurie. Instead, they were more worried about the team and were willing to help each other."

The 2006 season had been something of a break-out year for Fa'asavalu after plodding along in the Academy and fringes of the first team squad. Bigger things were always anticipated when he and big wing Dominic Feaunati signed in the afterglow of some stunning performances for Samoa in the 2003 World Cup in Australia. Despite producing a man of the match performance against England in that tournament, no offers came in from union outfits in Europe or Australia and New Zealand. The call from Saints' then boss Ian Millward was the only offer on the table – Fa'asavalu had no choice but to try and make the difficult transfer to the other side of the world and get to grips with a whole new ball game.

Both Samoans made their debuts in a youthful Saints team on a freezing cold Sunday afternoon up at Barrow – a day in which the PA announcer decided to duck reading out the pair's names, opting to pass the microphone over to Ian Bridge for the then Saints press officer to pronounce.

Feaunati made a more explosive initial impact, with his flying fists playing a prominent role in the infamous Good Friday brawl against Wigan which copped a three-match ban from the disciplinary and appeared to be denounced as a "shithouse" by Wigan skipper Andrew Farrell. He was back in time to win a Challenge Cup medal, but then his career at Saints took a downward spiral and he left for Leigh and then returned to union: all this before his compatriot had really been given a chance to make his presence felt in the first team.

It was always felt that as a forward it would take Fa'asavalu longer to adjust than the wingman who largely had the same job in both codes. It had taken Perelini, who had made a similar journey in 1994, a few months to find his feet – albeit in a part time age. But into the second year of his contract there must have been a few scratching their heads wondering whether he was suited to the 13-man code.

Fa'asavalu was among them and some years later, he told the *Independent* newspaper how that all altered with Daniel

Anderson's arrival in May 2005.

He said: "I was lost; I just didn't get it. Daniel said to me: 'If you agree to stay here, I'll teach you to play.' That was the deal he offered, and I put my faith in him. From then on, I started to achieve. We won everything there was to win in 2006 and reached the Super League final every year after that."

Fa'asavalu looked like a new man – and despite not being a real giant, in short bursts he played like a cross between the Incredible Hulk and Rambo. In the March of that season he really showed that he was now a different player, showing how much he had developed in a short space of time under Anderson's tutelage.

Speaking after giving the prop a rare start in the cup game against Doncaster Lakers, Anderson was delighted with the two-tries and energetic display he got back in return.

"One of the highlights of Friday's game was the performance of Maurie Fa'asavalu. When you see his bullocking, barnstorming runs I am as entertained as any of those spectators standing on the opposite side of the field to me.

"He is improving his length of time on the field, and is now averaging 15-20 carries a game and a similar number of tackles per match.

"He could not do that last year. All credit should go to Maurie for getting in shape that has allowed him to do more for us.

"Maurie is keen to do analysis on his own game and ask questions of the coaching staff to improve himself. He jumps into every training session and is keen to learn and listens attentively to the more experienced front rowers like Paul Anderson, Jason Cayless and Nick Fozzard. And in general nobody likes to be matched up against him when we do contact work because he is all bone and has a natural power about him."

That year he reaped the rewards for his endeavour – and capped the post match celebrations after the Challenge Cup and Grand Final with a celebratory Samoan war dance.

Fellow impact prop forward James Graham gave a strong taste of what an outstanding front rower he was going to develop into. Then aged just 20, he became the youngest club skipper for a long time when he took the armband to lead a youthful team to a narrow loss in Catalan. To cut it in the front row, mixing it with grizzled, hard-nosed mature blokes who know all the dark arts of front row play, took some doing. But he passed the test with flying colours, earning a Great Britain call up for the test match with the Kiwis at Knowsley Road and being picked for, but missing out with a broken hand, the Tri-Nations tour Down Under.

He was no nonsense, two carries a set metre maker – one who back then looked destined to go on to even greater things, not least because of the strings he was adding to his bow. His work with the technical adviser Alan Wilson enabled the flame-haired front rower from Maghull to develop his ball-playing attributes. It was a breath of fresh air to see a 20-year-old displaying the ball-playing skills of a 32-year-old Brian Lockwood.

Born and raised in football-mad Maghull, a small town between Liverpool and Ormskirk, Graham was drawn to the game courtesy of his Cumbrian born father. He had progressed through the junior ranks, gaining international honours for England Academy in series wins over Australia, with Graham captaining the side that claimed a famous victory on Australian soil.

2005 had proved to be a real breakthrough season for the former Blackbrook Royal, making 27 appearances and being named Saints' Young Player of the Year, for his mature, powerful performances. Super League XI would be even better.

Both Graham and Fa'asavalu had two other battle-hardened props in the ranks to learn their trade off – Cayless and Fozzard. Daniel Anderson knew exactly what he was getting in Cayless.

"Jason will add size, strength and dynamism to our pack which will be fearsome next season. He will fit our style of play perfectly and will improve our overall physicality and skill levels," he said.

Cayless certainly did that in that first year, but alas the last two years of his contract at Knowsley Road were wrecked by injury.

Speaking in his last interview in England before heading back to Sydney, in September 2009 Cayless spoke of his regret and pleasure at time spent at Knowsley Road.

He said: "My first year in 2006 was unbelievable – we won everything that was on offer. We have won so much, particularly in the first year, that it is hard to pin it down to one highlight.

"On a professional level, I'll miss the team and the boys here. Once you have done that and have a history it is hard to leave it behind and walk away.

"They are a great team and club – on a personal level they are a great bunch of lads too.

"I have really enjoyed my time here, the town has been great and the St Helens people are lovely. They are so enthusiastic and love their rugby – there has not been a downside to being here apart from being injured."

Paul Wellens again observed how that full complement of props had contributed that year, and speculated on the monetary value of that contingent in today's game.

Wellens said: "Daniel had seen Jammer play and then not feature for a while and asked why, so he was straight back in for his first game at Leeds in 2005. He also looked and said 'Who is this Maurie guy? Get him in!'

"Our big lads were not only big, they were good rugby players too. If they were to come back on the market now they would command massive salaries, big money. Imagine what Paul Anderson and Jason Cayless, in his prime, would command. And obviously James Graham is in the NRL. Even Nick Fozzard, who was not even getting in the team for the finals, was in the Great Britain squad in 2005 and playing well. Every club would be after those props."

16

August

The countdown to Twickenham started no sooner had the final hooter sounded at Huddersfield. A shock result in the other semi-final saw the Giants beat Leeds at Odsal and therefore hand Saints what on paper looked like easier opposition, if less eye-catching. Saints had cup final history dating back to Wembley 1978 – and a few were disappointed not to be getting the chance of vengeance for that game that was lost courtesy of a Derek Noonan knock on.

But that did not stop cup final fever taking a hold with fans queuing in miserable weather to buy their Twickenham tickets as soon as they went on sale. Coach Daniel Anderson said: "I've never seen this before, it is amazing. Obviously there is quite a warm feeling in the club at the moment. And those fans of ours are real troopers. It's astonishing."

Cup final fever spread into the dressing room with chants of "Armani!" echoing in the dressing room after the semi success – a reference to the type of suits the squad were hoping to be measured up for – is perhaps one of the more unusual victory songs for a celebrating rugby league team.

Huddersfield's shock victory did present Saints with a slight problem, in the sense that it meant that they would be the only club still with a twin, even triple, competition focus going through the month of August. Ironically Giants would be Saints' opponents in that first game back on the campaign trail. With Saints having a six-point cushion at the Super League summit and the cup final several weeks away, some suggested that Anderson could leave players out during August's games, to help keep the top squad fresh.

But you sensed he was already working backwards from

Twickenham in calculating if, where and when he could afford to send a depleted team – the long trip to the south of France was already jumping up and down with bells on. Maybe there was a desire to get through the month unscathed to buy that luxury and room to manoeuvre.

However, the other aspect to factor in was that 20 into 17 just wasn't going to go and competition was intensified sharply with skipper Paul Sculthorpe, who missed the semi-final, champing at the bit to make the final. There was clearly going to be an almighty battle for spots and a selection headache for the boss.

"With the Catalans game on the week before the cup final I will ensure we take a team that is very competitive. But I also have to ensure the preparation for the final isn't hampered or obstructed by factors such as the searing heat and travel, because the Challenge Cup is a very prestigious trophy and we need to show respect to that competition."

One sideline that needed putting to bed first, however, was speculation that Daniel Anderson was to quit Knowsley Road at the end of that season with reports suggesting he would return Down Under because his young family was homesick. Anderson was forced to reiterate his intention to see out a contract that ran until the end of the 2007 season – something he ended up doing and then adding another year for good measure.

He said: "My family has moved through a couple of countries now and there will be a time when we will go home, but I have not said to anybody I am going home at the end of this year. We have some good young players here and sometimes you don't want to leave a squad when you know that good times are coming. There are some outstanding players here and I'm really enjoying working with them."

Good times were indeed coming but it was back to bread and butter before any champagne corks would be popping. And that started with Saints thumping Huddersfield 56-8 – a game which underlined clearly that the men in the red vee had a twin track focus whereas the Fartowners had eyes only on the cup.

It was a match in which Paul Anderson, who joined the Giants coaching staff at the end of that season, started his tuition with a hands-on demonstration. In yet another barnstorming performance, the heavyweight prop robustly carted the ball into the thick of the battle, regularly carrying tacklers with him as he smashed holes in the visitors' defensive line.

Baloo's performance was just one element of a commanding team display, as ruthless Saints rattled in ten tries to put down a calling card in advance of the Challenge Cup Final.

Although both sides came into the game on the back of semi-final victories, only one team was still seeing champagne corks popping from the previous weekend's success.

Added to that the Giants left out four key players – and they were always going to be a different proposition with big man Eorl Crabtree adding power to their ranks.

Coach Daniel Anderson said the result gave no insight into the final, adding: "I don't think Huddersfield were really there mentally and we won't be reading too much into this result. We scored some nice tries and that was good for morale and for our scoring difference in the table but it won't have much credence for Twickenham."

That said, Huddersfield trudged off at the end of a half-century mauling knowing fully well that Saints were capable of getting better for the Twickenham showdown once absentees Sean Long and Jason Hooper were back on board.

Anderson said: "We played our style of game, but Huddersfield did not play theirs. We won the game and got two points and it has lodged into our opponents' minds just what a potent attacking team we are."

Saints may have been measured up for their Twickenham suits and were sitting six points clear at the Super League summit, but there was no resting on laurels. With competition for places intensified by the return of Sculthorpe and shortly Jason Hooper, it was clear two senior forwards from the regular panel were going to miss out for the final. All seemed keen for it not to be them and packmen Vinnie Anderson, Jon Wilkin and Maurie Fa'asavalu were prominent in the late flourish which brought up the half century.

The coach knew what was coming – and barring injury – he was going to have a tough call, but that went with the territory. He said: "I have got absolutely no qualms about any of the forwards I put out on to the field, so when it comes to making a decision, players will miss out who are in good form, which may seem hard to swallow. But that is the way it is because of the talent we have available here.

"Selection will ultimately be about the balance of our team and selecting the best 17 to do the job of beating Huddersfield in a cup final. Although there are two matches to play before then, I would not think that too many players, because of their current form, have got anything additional to showcase in the next two weeks.

"Most players are playing the style and brand of football that they enjoy, and they are showing their skills and versatility week in, week out. That just leaves me with the problem of breaking the bad news to those players who will have to miss out – but unfortunately I have to pick 17 players, not 19 or 20."

Next on the agenda was a trip to Wheldon Road – or the Jungle as it was then christened – and a tough examination was expected against a team that was battling for their Super League survival. Anderson commented that even the league's off colour, struggling out of form sides had been raising their game when the Saints were in town.

Anderson said: "Whether it was Wakefield at Belle Vue or Salford at the Willows – it does not matter who we play, their form picks up against us, and expect that to be the same this weekend." I understand the Jungle can be quite an intense atmosphere, but I really enjoy that. I am a rugby league man through and through and have had some wonderful experiences at our opposition's venues.

"The Willows is a hostile place to visit, but I had a bit of a smirk on my face when they throw some lines at you coming down the tunnel. I expect Castleford to be a similar experience. We expect a hard, tough, torrid encounter because they have a pretty bruising style of play. When we played them here it was quite a physical encounter."

It was anything but a torrid test with Saints romping to a 72-4 with 12 tries, all converted by the faultless boot of Jamie Lyon, breaking two club Super League match records with 12 goals and 32 points. Not only was the attacking machine ticking over nicely, with Leon Pryce prominent in five of Saints' half dozen first half tries, but the defence was again at its stingiest best. No player illustrated that defensive tenacity as much as Sean Long – playing with strapping after missing three out of the previous four games – as he frequently got back to make some telling last ditch tackles.

Anderson said: "We have worked very hard on our defence and are very proud of how few points we have conceded this year. Our position in the table is a reward for our defensive intensity. It is fair to say that our defence has noticeably tightened in recent weeks, prior to that we had a spell where we conceded a lot of points against Harlequins, Wakefield and Catalans.

"After the Harlequins game, we had a team meeting and showed our season average for defence was 14 but in those three games, we let in 28 points per game. It was in the week prior to the Leeds game at Headingley that we made a goal to return to our season average and since that meeting we have let in 14 (v Leeds), 0 (v Hull KR), 8 (v Huddersfield) and 4 (v Castleford)."

Saints had a problem seven days ahead of their cup final appearance having been given the short straw of a trip to Stade Saint Michel in Canet to tackle the Catalans for the second time that season on foreign soil.

It was a problem game Saints had anticipated when the fixtures were initially published and had called Catalans with a view to switching their game with Saints' home game in July, but there was no ground available and that move fell through.

Saints had to use a Plan B and their six point cushion at the top of the table and a healthy squad gave Daniel Anderson options seven days before Twickenham. It looked a no brainer of a decision.

Now the club had form under the Millward era for sending out under-strength teams, especially in the run up to cup finals, with the scandal of the Bradford match hitting the club in 2002. The game at Valley Parade, in which Millward left out 12 first teamers and played the last 25 minutes a man short, was viewed as a real black mark against Saints' name. It led to all kinds of inquiries and demands that Saints produce doctor's notes to explain the absence of so many players. It also saw Bradford chairman Chris Caisley demand that Saints be hit hard with something more substantial than a "two and sixpence fine". It wrecked Saints' build up to the 2002 final and they were underdone and undone by Wigan the following week at Murrayfield.

Four years later Daniel Anderson took a clearly calculated decision not to risk sending his top squad to France – and the performance of those lads ensured that there was not even a murmur of criticism.

Ahead of the game, he explained: "We want to perform to the best of our abilities in that showpiece event at Twickenham and we would not be able to do that if we sent the first team squad to Catalans. The bottom line is that a trek to the South of France is a difficult travelling trip when you add together the time at airports, flights and transfers.

"I am sure not everyone will agree with the club's decision, but I owe it to our fans, sponsors and rugby league that we are at 100 per cent for the blue riband event that the Challenge Cup represents. I never show any disrespect to rugby league or want to trivialise Super League fixtures but this is the sensible and logical decision."

Apollo Perelini and Matt Viljoen stayed behind to train and treat the players not making the trip, with Anderson, technical adviser Alan Wilson and high performance manager Mike Rush going out with a team that the coach had real confidence in.

Speaking ahead of the trip Anderson said: "We have given opportunities to some very exciting young players who also are all local lads. Players like Dean McGilvray, Steven Bannister, Paul Clough, Matt Smith and Scott Moore have all represented Saints at Super League level or are members of the Great Britain Under 18s.

"Players like Paul Leyland, Gaz Langley, Craig Littler, Ian Webster and Neil Rigby have been playing for Saints in the age group competitions for a number of years and will be very proud to don the red vee for the first time.

"There is a balance in the side, with a few older heads and internationals in there. In Tommy Hodgkinson's case he has probably been the best performer in the Academy competition. He is great team player whose form has been consistently of top quality, and he replaces Paul Anderson as the old, hard head in the team.

"Although it will be tough and we will have to play well, we are going there to win the game and the extra carrot is that we can wrap up the League Leaders' Shield. But the bottom line is we have a blue riband event on Saturday week. Ahead of that the staff will be assembling here at 3.30am on Friday to get on a bus to the airport to get to Perpignan and then we return on Sunday afternoon.

"From my experience at New Zealand Warriors, travel does take it out of you so when we return the players will need a day off to recover and then we have to train and prepare for the cup final. Then we have to leave for London possibly on Wednesday or Thursday, so that leaves us with one or two days. Then you add the heightened security at the moment and the outside chance of delays or cancellations on flights.

"I owe it to the club and fans to make sure we are at our peak physically and mentally for the Challenge Cup Final and it makes it logical that this is the way we have to go. If we were in the UK playing a game it would be different, but the travel is the problem."

Unlike the lame surrenders at Bradford in 2002 and 2004, this performance said everything about the culture permeating through the club in 2006. And that was embodied by 20-year-old James Graham, who was Saints' youngest captain of recent times, leading a youthful charge.

He was swelling with pride when he beamed: "To be captain of a club like this, even if it is just for one game, is a real honour."

However, the coach revealed that this was not the first time he had led the club in a senior match.

"He has acted as captain in the past when I have taken players off. And I have a huge opinion of James as a leader in this organisation. This is a natural step for him and he has the instincts and natural qualities of a leader," Anderson said.

It was not all about youth – there was a shock recall for veteran forward Tommy Hodgkinson, who last played for Saints in 1994 before moving to Bradford. In a colourful career that also took in amateur sides Haydock and Thatto Heath, Hodgkinson played professionally with Widnes, Oldham, Lancashire Lynx, Swinton, Rochdale and Blackpool.

The then 36-year-old was brought back to Saints to be an 'old head' in the Academy set up where he impressed the coaching staff with his attitude. Coach Anderson had no qualms about bringing him into the first team picture.

"He is one of the best players in the Academy competition – I am not fazed about ages, just form. We have some young inexperienced players in there, but there are also some internationals in there," he said.

Although Saints lost 26-22, it was a mighty close affair and a game they would have won with a cooler head at the end when they conceded a late try.

Anderson said: "We scrambled well, hit hard and deserved to win the game in the end. But class players like Stacey Jones, invariably get teams out of trouble and that is what he did for Catalans. Every single member of our team made a contribution, with some big plays too, but it was those five senior players who really kept us there or thereabouts for the whole game.

"Those players – Ian Hardman, Vinnie Anderson, Lee Gilmour, James Graham and Nick Fozzard were the glue that held the team together. They definitely provided enough inspirational moments in the game to keep our youngsters going forward."

17

Challenge Cup Final

The 2006 Challenge Cup Final should have been the first to have been held at the new Wembley. It had been marketed as such by the RFL from the previous autumn. Alas, delays in construction meant that the RFL took the decision in spring to switch the showpiece event to Twickenham, never the most popular of the game's on the road venues between 2000 and 2006. They had got themselves boxed in, having advertised London as the venue, with 30,000 neutrals already booking tickets. And to further throw a spanner in the works, Cardiff's Millennium Stadium – scene of Saints' previous cup final win over Wigan – was already booked out to the Rolling Stones. So the not quite fully finished Twickenham it was, scene of Saints' tactical kicking 2001 triumph over Bradford in a game that, to put politely, was one for the purists. It was nevertheless a final win against a very strong Bulls side and the way that final is often dismissively regarded by some fans in a way says everything about how the post-1996 generation had become blasé about success.

Twickenham was not Wembley, but the Challenge Cup trophy was still something special despite it getting knocked about since the switch to summer and the subsequent 'bigging up' of the Super League Grand Final at Old Trafford. True, it was not like the old days when fans would be singing the full range of Wembley songs and the town would be bedecked in red and white for six weeks before the big day. 'Que sera, sera, whatever will be, will be, we're going to Twickenham' does not scan in the same way.

And nor was the dislike of the RFU top brass for past misdemeanours a side issue for some. Although both games had moved on, the gangway between codes was now free, for good or ill, some league fans still would have liked something resembling a truth and reconciliation commission before moving on and throwing their hard earned coin into the coffers of HQ.

It was nonetheless a significant date – and Saints needed that first pot on the shelves, a first major trophy since Ian Millward's departure and something to physically recognise how superior they were – something that did not happen the year before despite walloping Wigan 75-0.

Daniel Anderson had a full strength squad to pick from – meaning his first massive call of the year and heartache for two in-form, seasoned professionals. In the week building up to the game Anderson said: "I cannot say anything negative about the players' form because every single player has contributed at a higher level for the last month. But I have to pick a team which will give us the best balance for the game to play against Huddersfield."

Huddersfield, coached by Jon Sharp, Millward's former assistant at Saints, had shocked Leeds to win the other semi-final and their forte was their big pack, but Saints were no shrinking violets themselves.

"They have a lot of big men, but we don't have a small team ourselves so we relish a physical challenge. Our players are keen to contest whatever physical side the game produces. Big games always bring extra effort and desperation from both teams. We pay respect to every team and we won't be perched on our ivory tower during the course of this week," Anderson said.

Keiron Cunningham, a veteran of all five of Saints' previous summer era cup final appearances, had been a dominant feature of the team's fine displays in steamrollering Doncaster, Bradford, Catalans and Hull KR en route to Twickenham.

Although hot-favourites, Cunningham was taking nothing for granted against the Giants, for whom his opposite number Brad Drew was marked a key man. Cunningham said: "We have basically got to go out and do what Daniel tells us but if we don't we will come unstuck. Huddersfield are a very good side, with massive forwards and some smart, quick backs. Chris Thorman and Brad Drew can run riot so we know who we have got to control and how we have to defend.

"We have to win the battle in the middle for starters because they will have some big lads coming at us. They play off the back of that big pack, particularly Thorman who is one of the most talented sixes around with a great kicking game."

Although it was Cunningham's sixth final – and he subsequently went on to make it to eight with just the one loss – he still had the same hunger as when he was a teenager playing in that 'Ultimate Comeback' final in 1996.

"To make a cup final is a dream for every player and all those previous ones mean something to me. I was only a kid for the first one and it was more shock than anything going out in front of a packed Wembley. At least I am more mature now and can handle the stage and the atmosphere a bit more.

"You still get nervous and get the jitters, but as an 18-year-old going into that Wembley roar it absolutely zaps everything. Your legs go, but now as a bit more of a senior pro I can handle things a bit better, especially the big games," he said.

Although the Thatto Heath-born hooker had won every domestic honour – World Club Challenges, Super League titles and Challenge Cups, for some reason the individual honours eluded him. Maybe it was because the level of Cunningham's weekly performances was so high; perhaps those voting took it for granted. Although when he did finally finish he was not short of recognition, with the town erecting a statue to salute him. But when he was still playing he did declare that he would have liked to have emulated his older brother and got his hands on the Lance Todd Trophy Eddie won in 1982.

Ahead of the Twickenham clash Cunningham said: "You cannot predict who wins the man of the match, it is just who plays well on the day. I would love to win it though. I have a nice little trophy cabinet at home with plenty of caps and winners medals. All that it is short of is a Lance Todd and a Man of Steel, so I will have to do my best over the next couple of years to try and get those."

Skipper Paul Sculthorpe had not collected the Lance Todd either, but he had won Man of Steel twice. All that strength of character had been tested during a frustrating, stop-start 12 months. After damaging his knee ligaments skippering Great Britain the previous June, Sculthorpe had proved his fitness to Daniel Anderson and got the nod to skipper the side at Twickenham. But he would be the first to admit that this was Sculthorpe-lite, with injuries and the effects of them either sidelining him or inhibiting his natural game.

But there was a determination to get out there and play, not simply wear a shirt, on the big day. Four days before the showpiece Sculthorpe said: "It was a big blow to get injured in the Test match. Even though I knew I would be fit for the final, as a player you want games under your belt. Daniel said to me 'I want you playing in two of the three before it'. "Sometimes you lose a bit of touch when you are not playing, but in those two games I felt really good with the ball."

Reverting to the second row berth he occupied in his first season at Saints in 1998, Sculthorpe had a relatively quiet start to the season. That, combined with his recent string of injuries, meant for the first time in his illustrious award-winning career at Knowsley Road there were murmurings as to whether the skipper should command a starting spot – views would have been unthinkable two or three years ago when he was ripping the opposition to shreds with class and tenacity. Sculthorpe was no quitter and his determination not to be written off at 28 meant he was like the spider in Robert the Bruce's cave, constantly getting off the rehab table to have another crack.

Sculthorpe said: "It has been stop-start for me over the last year. But that was a major operation I went through last year, which took more healing than I probably realised, but hopefully I can put that behind me because I still have a lot of years ahead of me. Players go through it – Keiron had it with his injuries, especially his elbow, but look at the way he is playing now. It is the nature of the game.

"Of course it is disappointing to miss games. The fans see you when you are not playing, and are frustrated, but they are not as gutted as me. Players are only good when they are on the field."

He was not downcast by the criticism, and fully understands Daniel Anderson's decision to take the number 13 spot off him that season.

"At the start of the year when I was struggling with my knee, moving laterally and stepping, Daniel told me to get back onto the field it would be better to run the straight lines in the second row. I have been doing that, but hopefully now I can get more opportunity to use the ball and get my kicking game going again. At the end of the day that is the way I play the game and if I see something that needs doing I will do it," Sculthorpe said.

Talking about the game in front of them the Saints skipper added: "We just have to focus on the main job in hand. Huddersfield are a fair team – they would not be in the final if they were not. They are big, but so are we. Whichever way they want to play it we know we have a quality side that if we play to our potential they will have to play very well to beat us."

There was plenty of anticipation – but that was probably felt keenest amongst the handful of players for whom this would be their first Challenge Cup Final. There were not that many – half a dozen – on the field who had not appeared at this stage of the competition before – only Francis Meli and Jamie Lyon in the backline, with Jason Cayless joining Maurie Fa'asavalu and young guns James Roby and James Graham in making their maiden final appearances.

That is not strictly true in the case of Roby and Graham – a pair who were hoping to get a few more minutes on the park than the previous time they played on Challenge Cup final day.

Although Twickenham was Roby's first senior final, both he and fellow big match debutant James Graham had played in the curtain raiser prior to the 1997 Wembley showpiece. Unfortunately that game between St Helens schools under 11s and Batley/Dewsbury was cut short to a dozen minutes following a bomb scare.

Roby said: "We were kept in the tunnel for ages and only played about six minutes each way. But despite that it was still a brilliant experience, and we were all grabbing clumps of the Wembley grass afterwards and stuffing it in our pockets because we were just excited kids."

That taste of the big match, together with the coaching and encouragement he had down at Blackbrook Royals and then up at Saints had helped spur the youngster on to returning to the cup final arena nine years later for the main event.

"It has been a big year for me. It is my first final and, if picked, I will be trying to take in as much as I can," he said.

Although a substitute, the spark he gave to the side when thrown into the fray ten minutes before half-time was one of the features of Saints' play that season. It did not go unnoticed and only an untimely knee injury cost him a Great Britain place earlier this season, after he had forced his way into Brian Noble's training squad.

He admitted to still learning his craft back then – but Roby had good teachers at Knowsley Road and expected to improve his game by getting pointers off Anderson and Cunningham, something that paid dividends in the long run.

Of course it was first time around for coach Daniel Anderson and although he was clearly excited at the prospect of being part of this great English showpiece, there was no shortage of trepidation. Ahead of the game he said: "The game is my first final in the English game and is quite exciting. I believe this appearance is a reward for what we have done this year. I know it does not give us any right to hold aloft a trophy, but at least we are there. We have made the final and hopefully we will finish the job on Saturday. Statistics have a brutality about them and they record final successes and not how well a team has been playing over the course of a year.

"We played very well last season, but despite playing fantastically well in the play-offs the bottom line is we simply did not have the players. At the moment our form is great, and we are rewarded for our consistency with a place in the Challenge Cup Final and a place on top of Super League, but in the end the statistics will only show who lifted the trophy.

"Huddersfield are a very big, aggressive and pretty ferocious team. Although they have had mixed form in the Super League since claiming their final spot, they thoroughly deserved to beat Leeds in the semi."

And come game day, steely Saints kept their nerve and withstood a ferocious early onslaught from the underdogs to collect their fifth Challenge Cup in 11 years, triumphing 42-12. Although Saints had to go on the ropes a few times in the opening quarter, they hung on, soaking up those early body blows and conceded just the one score to wing Martin Aspinwall.

But once they finally got their hands on the ball in Giants territory they countered with sheer ruthlessness. Saints' superior fitness, big match experience, strength in depth, skill and game-breaking quality suddenly began to tell.

The result was never in doubt once Sean Long scampered over following fine work from Jamie Lyon and Ade Gardner four minutes before the break. This came after Willie Talau had settled the nerves with an equalising try off skipper Paul Sculthorpe's grubber.

The Giants executed their game plan to perfection and they had a gift in the opening seconds when Chris Thorman's spiralling kick off was fluffed by Leon Pryce and was gleefully collected by a grateful member of the claret and gold wave that was already up there in numbers.

The Giants' tails were up and they pounded the Saints line for what effectively amounted to three successive sets of six. Even when Saints got the ball back, the Giants defence was up to force an unusually ponderous Keiron Cunningham back over the line to force a goal line drop out.

This is where Saints spent the greater part of the first quarter as Thorman, Robbie Paul and Giants linchpin Brad Drew kept drilling the ball deep. It meant Saints' back three of Paul Wellens, Ade Gardner and Francis Meli were constantly having to cart the ball back off their own 'spongy' line – and the favourites were rarely able to get over the half way line with the ball. Had Saints become impatient, the error count would have mounted and Giants would have been able to cash in with more points which could have changed the game's complexion. But at the back Wellens broke their hearts by defusing a number of awkward kicks behind the line, and then reinforcements from the Saints bench gave Huddersfield something to think about in the 10 minutes each side of the break.

Faced with James Roby's nippiness at dummy half, the Giants

suddenly looked cumbersome and they simply could not hold Maurie Fa'asavalu, whose powerful surges punched gaping holes in the heart of the Huddersfield defence.

The explosive Samoan really hit his straps four minutes after the break when his blockbusting run left a trail of Fartowners in his wake in a 40-metre charge. The supporting Roby would have scored himself had he not been obstructed, but the youngster kept going, took the pass and was halted just short. Simple, cool headed rugby saw Wellens shovel the ball inside from the play the ball to send the bloodied Jon Wilkin charging over for the first of his brace of scores.

Despite his broken nose, suffered in the sixth minute, Wilkin toiled valiantly but his mixed day was complete when he was placed on report for an alleged high tackle on Giants wing Stuart Donlan. Further tries from Fa'asavalu, Lyon and Jason Cayless completed the rout as Saints turned the screw. Of those Lyon's touchdown perhaps summed up the huge gulf in class between the sides – and was possibly the clincher in giving Long the Lance Todd. The Saints number seven burst through on the half way and found the support cut off to his right. But he kept running and just as the defence was about to close him down Long had the presence of mind and ability to find Lyon out wide with an inch-perfect cross kick. Lyon swooped and despite the attention of Robbie Paul, was able to ground.

The referee wanted a second look – it was worth one, not to check the validity of it, more to marvel at the skill displayed! By this stage the magnificent contingent of Saints followers packed into the North Stand and other pockets around the ground were already celebrating a victory not diminished by it being against Huddersfield, rather than Leeds, Bradford or Wigan.

In fact the only thing that was second class about the proceedings was the trophy presentation. It was bad enough for the fans and players having to wait an age for the podium to be assembled instead of climbing the traditional steps. But the handover went off half cock, when guest of honour Martin Offiah scarpered to avoid getting his suit stained by the explosion of bubbly from the players behind him. As a result the most famous old trophy in rugby league was presented with as much gravitas as the prize giving at a holiday camp knobbly knees competition.

Having soaked it all in, the pre-match, the game and the celebrations, coach Anderson gave his verdict on the whole experience of being a Challenge Cup winner for the first time. It was something he would get used to, going on to guide Saints to the next two at Wembley.

He said: "The Challenge Cup Final experience at Twickenham has furnished me with memories that I will cherish. It was an overwhelming experience, which went beyond all my expectations. My highlight was walking out on to the pitch behind Tom van Vollenhoven, with the hairs on the back of my neck standing up with the level of noise entering the arena.

"It was a great day, with the general excitement of the game, followed by a proud and enjoyable post match. I have been absolutely astounded by the commitment of the players this year and this trophy is a just reward for them. It was good to get that first piece of silverware on the sideboard. Although everyone at St Helens recognises that this is a very good team across the board – the players value their team-mates and I am sure our spectators value the team – it is not until you win a trophy that the statistics and history will recognise your worth as a team. In saying this, we are determined that this is not our only success in 2006.

"We prepared very well for the game, but there was still a little bit of tension and apprehension in our game as a result of being overwhelming favourites. We know we are very good, but in any future big games I envisage you will see a more relaxed St Helens team. Plus everyone now has big match experience. Although we were down 6-0, we then kept our try line clean for the next 60 minutes. The resilience, skill, competitive nature of our players and the desire not to be the person to break our team defensive line meant that we won the game. We also had players coming off the bench who helped maintain our performance at such a high level, which simply broke Huddersfield in the end.

"It was a tough game and I have to admit that for Huddersfield to get the ball back after three seconds from their kick off was a little worrying. It was a tough start but I did not feel nervous because we were playing a really good game. We were rattled and bustled in the first 15 minutes, but that is what happens in big games, but we hung in there and got on with our game after this frenzied period. The big in-goal areas and the newly laid turf meant not a single kick went dead, which made it difficult, but it was the same for both teams.

"There is a genuine 20-25 man squad here at Knowsley Road and the contribution of everyone has put us where we are today. We have set a standard and there is a genuine desire to play in the red vee."

18

Jon Wilkin – One Man and his Bandage

One of the iconic images of the 2006 campaign – specifically the Challenge Cup victory – was that of a bloodied Jon Wilkin, with his nose held in place by an elaborately constructed bandage, blowing a kiss to the camera after scoring the second of his tries at Twickenham.

These days Wilkin has many facets to his game on and off the pitch; a fully fledged Test forward, a dependable figurehead in the Saints side during some subsequent tough years, a spokesman for the players union, an articulate television pundit and an occasional face on BBC's Question of Sport. But back then Wilkin, aged just 22, was starting his first ever final and was still consolidating his position in a highly competitive pack. Twickenham 2006 was probably a landmark game for him. The boy from east Hull had an absolute blinder in the thick of it against the Giants and had he stayed on the field for longer would have given Sean Long a real run for his money for the Lance Todd.

Speaking seven years after that win over Huddersfield Giants, Wilkin recalls with pride being part of the team that brought the first leg of the domestic treble home to Knowsley Road. And as a long-time admirer of the Challenge Cup he was still especially delighted that he could contribute to the rich tapestry of the most traditional of rugby league knock-out competitions.

Wilkin said: "As a young guy the Challenge Cup was the only trophy I had an awareness of, and I remember sitting around with my family watching the Wembley finals. As I became a lover of the game the footage I recall was never of the team winning the league title or the other cups, the iconic moment of any year was the captain lifting that big trophy at Wembley.

"In your career you like to be attached to the iconic moments within the season – the Challenge Cup Final was the iconic moment of the year. The Super League Grand Final at Old Trafford will get that history behind it eventually, but the Cup is special – you only have to look at the previous winners when the trophy is in your hands to pick that history up. When you touch it you recall every single key moment of the past – Don Fox, Sheffield Eagles beating Wigan, the '96 Ultimate Comeback. As a sportsman you would give anything to be attached to that trophy – it was a privilege to be in a position to lift it once, as I did as a substitute in 2004, but once you have done it, the appetite is there to lift it again and again."

Wilkin explained that there was some special motivation going into this game, having been thoroughly disappointed with how the previous year's cup campaign had ended. Falling at the last hurdle is tough, but for former Rover Wilkin flopping against the Black and Whites, his boyhood arch-enemies, probably rubbed some really coarse rock salt into those wounds.

However, Wilkin revealed that the wounds he had back then in 2005 were real, so much so that he should not have even been on the field, but his attachment to the cup and a bit of mind over matter meant he ran out with a balloon of a knee. And of course big games have a habit of finding out injuries, but that Hull defeat was not really down to that. Even coach Daniel Anderson put his hands up for a team being under-prepared that day.

But what doesn't kill you makes you stronger and Saints used the motivation and the lessons from that knockout when they had a chance to redeem themselves.

Wilkin explained: "The 2006 Cup final was certainly special for me. The Hull semi the previous year was a tough game. I remember going into that game and my knee was twice the size of what it should have been. I remember just about getting out of the dressing rooms to limp on to the field. That is how much the cup meant. It was about pushing through the boundary of pain – but I should not have played. It was such a disappointing day at Huddersfield – we had played so well leading up to the game, putting 75 points on Wigan, but then we produced one stinking performance.

"In sport you remember the bad games more than the good games. You ask me about any other cup semi-final – and there have been plenty – and I can't remember a single second. But ask me about that Hull game of 2005 and I can tell you every second of that match and the reasons why we lost. That is strange – it is the human mind. You are scarred by defeat. There is a recoil mechanism and a natural reaction to do better as a result."

The first chance to do better came with the 2006 Challenge Cup run.

"There was a nice pressure that we needed to win some trophies, and also Daniel had come in and he was meticulous and the delivery of everything he did and in such detail but he was quite relaxed in his style. That time there was pressure – but as one of relatively younger guys in the team, who had just got a first taste of international rugby, I was happy where I was sitting. It is difficult to think of anything but fond memories of that time. You are aware of pressure on the club. That is why you sign here – you want to be attached to the pressure that this club has, although we were well aware that since Ian Millward had gone we had not won a cup. As players you want to contribute to the timeline of the club in the brief time that our paths cross – every year you are aware of having an impact."

That year the class of 2006 certainly had an impact. And for the players, Wilkin taking it to Twickenham took none of the shine off the triumph despite what some fans and the media thought.

"Twickenham may have been an issue for the media and the fans but for players it is a cup final; and it could be anywhere, the magnitude of the game. I had already played at Cardiff as a sub in the 2004 final – the final had been on the road for six years. The stadium was fine but all we were thinking of was building up to it and that we had a good opportunity to win because we were a better team by some way. Man for man we were way better than Huddersfield in every position, that brings its own pressure and stresses. It becomes a purely individual thing to perform. When a team is expected to win it brings its own challenges and many teams have fallen foul of that pressure.

"I remember in the hotel the day before the game there was a crippling undercurrent of expectation from everyone, an understanding among the players that it was down to us. For Huddersfield they had quite simple preparation – play and enjoy the experience and if they win it is an absolute bonus. Even the Huddersfield fans there that day expected Saints to win," he said.

Ahead of the game, Saints gave a large nod back to tradition and invited Tom van Vollenhoven, the legendary South African and star of the late 50s and 60s teams, over to present their shirts on the eve of the game. Wilkin was honoured to get his jersey from such a man, but pre-match butterflies meant that he was slightly distracted and did not really appreciate it.

He said: "It was a smart move by the club at the time. There is a timeline upon which iconic people appear – one is Tom van Vollenhoven, just like Mal Meninga who did the honours a year later. When you meet these guys it is a great honour and bond you share – the red vee of the Saints plus the club ethos of friendship and community. That is what was so special to get that shirt off Tom. However, that stage the night before the game it is one of the last things you want to be doing because your mind is elsewhere. It is hard to enjoy it at that time – but nevertheless it was a huge honour to be handed a Saints shirt any match but to get it from Tom the night before the Cup final is special."

Wilkin was right, Saints on paper were head and shoulders about the Giants – strange to say given the Yorkshire side featured two leviathans in Eorl Crabtree and Wayne McDonald in the front row. Under the stewardship of Ken Davey Huddersfield had slowly been building their side – this one would get better in the years to come. But the Giants' breed of 2006 was an abrasive, weighty unit whose level was greater than the sum of its parts.

Wilkin said: "They were a difficult team to play at the time and had a really good crack at us, but we had too much quality and fitness. That time we just seemed to steamroller teams – in that game we had Lee Gilmour, James Roby, James Graham and Maurie Fa'asavalu coming off the bench – we had real impact.

"Keiron was absolutely immense, he was unbelievable. His stats were tremendous at Twickenham, and we had a couple of guys in the team who played the ball really quickly so my job was to follow Keiron around.

"I can't recall what position I was actually playing. I obviously got knocked out in the first half and got my nose busted. I think I was down to play left back row but ended up playing in the middle of the field. Daniel quite liked me in the middle anyway and so naturally shuffled me around. A lot of my success in the early part of my career was due to Keiron. I could sense when he was running, and knew where to be. When Keiron jumped out of dummy half right I knew he was going to come back off his right foot to the left. If I could appear behind that ruck then I would get there. Similarly if he jumped out to his left he would try and beat those markers and square up and there would be a hole outside. A lot of the earlier part of my career when I was making breaks and punching holes – more than I do now – was as a result of that. The game has changed.

"My second try was like that. Keiron jumped out of dummy half and I sort of had an instinct what he was going to do. He beat the markers and I was running across play to their tired defenders. That was a bit of a plan to do that – Keiron kept running and I just did likewise and just changed my line of running. Those guys I was targeting had clocked off in the middle of the field and I found myself in some space.

"I scored that try and could not breathe because I had two tampons up my nostrils to stem the blood flow. I remember scoring and lying on the floor absolutely exhausted. I could not breathe out of my nose but every time I breathed in I was gargling blood at the back of my throat. I felt like I was essentially drowning on the pitch for 20 minutes of that second half."

It turned out well for Wilkin, but for a good while the accidental crack he had taken from Paul Anderson's head looked as though it had ended his afternoon before it had really begun. If there was one bloke whose head you don't want planting in the middle of your face it is 19st Baloo. The initial pain was the least of Wilkin's worries – the big battle was stemming the blood flow.

Wilkin explained: "I thought it was game over. All that time I kept thinking that my performances had been improving all year and I was contributing lots to the team. You are defined by iconic moments in cup finals and I didn't want mine to be defined by the fact that I had played five minutes and then badly broken my nose.

"I got into the changing room and looked in the mirror and it was a mess, my nose was sideways, plastered all over my face and it was moving, not attached, and floating around really. Our club doctor Simon Perret knew exactly what to do. He put Vaseline on his fingers and shoved them up my nose and straightened it. He has the biggest fingers you have seen, so it was a traumatic experience, but he managed to straighten it. He said 'we need to stop the blood'. True, we did need to do that because I was bleeding ridiculous amounts. Then he said if we can stop the blood you can get back on. A light went on – from that moment I was thinking 'brilliant' because mentally since leaving the pitch I was switching off and suddenly that light went back on. I said 'get it strapped up and get me back on'.

"I went back on but that was not the end of it. I got blood-binned a couple more times, with one of them coming after Maurie Fa'asavalu had made a break and I was up in support. I broke the line but when Huddersfield's full back Paul Reilly tackled me, one of the tampons flew out of my nose and blood just squirted out everywhere and all over my top. Their players were not stupid, they were saying to the ref 'he's bleeding, get him off!' And at that point I am thinking 'my day is not far off done here'. But the medical team were amazing that afternoon. Simon has put me on the field in so many games when by right I ought not to be out there, but he understands and would never put a player in danger. He also understood how important that Challenge Cup Final was. It was not about having a straight nose, it was about being out there and being part of a successful team and winning the Challenge Cup.

"That is the sort of relationship I have always had with Simon. He knows me and what I want and he can tell when I am seriously hurt. I really enjoy working with him."

In boxing you occasionally see a fighter get a cut so bad in the early rounds that he knows he has limited time to stop his opponent before the referee jumps in. Although it is not headless chicken stuff, you see the injured fighter throw absolutely everything into the bout. At Twickenham that is what you saw from Wilkin for about 30 minutes of that game.

Wilkin was philosophical amidst the blood, snot, flying tampons, bandages and gamesmanship. He said: "It focused me into thinking the time you get to spend on a field is tiny as a part of your life. It is hard because I thought my time was done – and then I got that reprieve to get back on and I thought 'I am not going to waste this chance'. Every minute and second of that was precious and maybe doing that to my nose was the good slap around the face I needed. At the time we were such a good team and we thought it was our right to get to those games, this is what we do, but I remember thinking it had been taken away and then when I went back on I was doing things that a coach wouldn't want me doing. I was supposed to be left back row but I was a nuisance and not sticking to where I should have been playing – I was flying out of the line trying to kill all of their players.

"I made a big effort on a kick chase and Stuart Donlan came out of dummy half and I walloped him. I thought it was a fair shoulder charge. I am not sure if was the knock to the head but I was doing stuff that had we lost the game then in the analysis afterwards I would have been hammered. Daniel was describing me as a lost dog – I did likewise in a play-off game against Leeds when I got knocked out five minutes into the game – and could not remember my name, but was running like a front rower."

And once he did get back on the field, he did make his mark, most notably when he crossed the whitewash. Describing the first try, Wilkin said: "I look back and a lot of tries I scored in my career have come from that kind of play. It is basically following up a good break and then a quick play the ball. At that stage if you draw a line in the air and run the law of averages says you will score and the person defending the line will not be able to stop you. When I put the ball down Wello and Jammer jumped on my back and I blew the kiss the camera. I love that picture because it

145

sums up my career looking back – it was Saints, the red vee and beside me were two of my best mates sharing the moment. It is one of my favourite pictures – it made all the nationals and the woman who took the photograph came and thanked me, saying thank you for blowing the kiss down my lens. I had not done it for the picture, rather I was more blowing it to my family and friends."

The remainder of the game was not without incident for the bloodied Wilkin, who was operating like a Duracell bunny. He even snapped up one of his trademark intercepts – a play which has subsequently been coached out of his game.

"After second try I thought I had made a mark and had contributed, not just scored my tries but led the team with some energy and intensity. I had done my job in energising and inspiring the lads. When I came off I was happy and it was only then that I heard people saying how well I had done.

"Alan Wilson, our technical adviser – a bloke whom I massively respected as a coach because he was so honest – came over and was really complimentary about my performance. I thought 'I must have had a good day today' then. "Sitting on the bench with the job done is such a good feeling. You have won the game and it is a lovely position to be in because that huge amount of pressure that has been on your head for months, leading up has gone. The weight just lifts.

"It was special. In 2005 I had forgotten my dad's birthday and so told him that I would get him a cup winner's medal for a belated present. So once I had been presented with it I went up and found him in the Twickenham crowd and gave it to him with the words 'happy birthday dad. Sorry I forgot it last year!'

"You share the moment of the game afterwards with the fans – I gave my socks away. Walking around after the game is the best feeling ever, seeing everyone unified and happy. As rugby players, professional sportsmen, we are lucky. Very few people in their jobs get to see the people they make happy. That is what makes entertainment so lovely – you get 30-40,000 people sharing your happiness."

19

Sean Long – the Last Voice before Kick Off

In 2006 Saints had a lot of big beasts in the ranks, plenty of massive personalities and team choc-a-block with star players with plenty of nous and knowhow. However, it was invariably the same voice that those players heard geeing them and barking the orders in the dressing room before heading down the tunnel. Sean Long – the linchpin of the team and the man tasked to call the shots by coach Daniel Anderson – was that person. And that season the enigmatic Wiganer was in his absolute element.

Everything had fallen into place for the master string-puller to work his magic – a big dominant pack to lay a platform, great service from dummy half, a dynamic number six and some real strike out wide. Maybe that year was not as clear-cut straightforward as a cursory glance down the playing roster suggests. Another factor that made it a stand-out season for Long was the way his 2005 had been so cruelly ended courtesy of Terry Newton's vicious, late, high tackle.

Victims of crime often speak of their unwillingness to leave the house after muggings or burglaries; assault victims particularly can understandably be a bit timid after being on the wrong end of a beating. With that in mind you do wonder how professional sportsmen mentally deal with the bad fouls, bordering on GBH, and bounce back up for more as soon as the bones have mended. After being clubbed by Newton's elbow/forearm Long had to have two metal plates inserted to repair his fractured cheekbone and was initially told it may take up to a year to regain full feeling in his face.

Given Long's prowess as a scrum half relied on him taking it to the line, running at the big fellas and being the go to man to put the big play on for the last tackle. Yet there was no visible flicker of half-heartedness or timidity from Long on his return – instead there was a sheer determination to grab back what was robbed from him at the end of a gruelling 2005 season – the chance of another Grand Final.

To be a top drawer scrum half – invariably being the smallest man on the field but the one charged with making the team tick – takes special characteristics. You think of classic half backs – Alex Murphy, Andy Gregory, Steve Nash and Bobbie Goulding – and you see pint sized guys whose faces would stand clogging. Hard-facedness, cheek and a brash sort of arrogance are invariably hallmarks of the bloke wearing the number seven. It probably helps if the incumbent has no fear of injury, has balls of steel or is just a little bit doolally. Longy, as some of his scrapes illustrate, could often appear to be daft as a brush – but what a shrewd footballer he was and one singled out for intelligence and earmarked as a future coach by Daniel Anderson.

When Long first joined Saints in June 1997 – a bargain £80,000 buy from neighbouring Widnes having been discarded by his hometown Wigan club – it was his blinding pace and support play that made him a stand-out prospect. The years rolled by and we had the lot, from a multitude of weird and wonderful haircuts from Mohican to dreads to some entertaining 'homecoming celebrations' which invariably saw him taking his trousers off. From the depths of despair with the serious 2001-ending knee injury sustained against Huddersfield to the height of elation of running around with St Bernard's head on after playing his part in the famous Wide to West try. Those poor kids had to turn away in disbelief with Long unmasking St Bernard and revealing a middle aged bloke with a bald head.

No player coped, nay revelled, in adversity and controversy as much as Long – and that was shown with the quality of rugby he played in the aftermath of the 2004 Easter Monday betting scandal. Having been left out of the team for the trip to Bradford, and having seen the 17 men and boys who Ian Millward was sending to Odsal, Long spied the chance to make a few easy bob and backed the Bulls on the coupon. *The Daily Mail* had a field day and once again rugby league became newsworthy. He was subsequently banned for three months, with partner-in-crime Martin Gleeson copping a longer penalty as he played in the same game, but not immediately. And although he copped a fair bit of booing and barracking from opposing fans it was water off a duck's back. Long guided Saints to Cardiff and then produced an utterly masterful Lance Todd-winning display to help conquer Wigan in the final while the Sword of Damocles was dangling above his head.

Whether it was hand-wringing editorials, barracking from the opposition or forearms to the face Long simply let it ride over him. And having spent years maturing from the quicksilver support player into a dominant, controlling number seven, Long began to lap up that extra responsibility. It was a responsibility that coach Daniel Anderson was only too keen to load upon his naturally gifted scrum half.

Anderson said: "I had been very fortunate to coach Stacey Jones at the Warriors and I had seen close up the big teams in the NRL. I had watched the big players in the big teams who dominated the landscape like Alfie Langer at Broncos and Freddie Fittler at Roosters – players who dominated their teams in the way they play. I wanted to replicate that with a dominant half back. I was a huge fan of 'if you had class half backs then they should be utilised.'

"In that first year we tweaked the team a fraction offensively. I want my teams to play through the half back so I was starting to give an enormous amount of responsibility to Longy, kicking and everything, and he took to it like a duck to water. I thought that was a key and again, like Keiron, he repaid me.

"Sometimes you can split your halves because not every scrum half can dominate a game – it is a demanding role but Longy flourished in it. He was at a time in his career when his absolute brilliant speed had diminished but that had been replaced a little bit and complemented by the top two inches. After that he became one of the most intelligent players in the game. I was here at the time when I said to him, 'You need to run this team!'"

And run it he did.

He also made history that season by becoming the first man to win the coveted Lance Todd Trophy three times. Long's kicking game in the win over Huddersfield was vital. He also grabbed a crucial try just before the break and set up two others with his boot to clinch the man of the match award ahead of runner-up Jon Wilkin, whose all action display earned him two tries, despite suffering a broken nose in the sixth minute.

But it was Long who got his name etched into the trophy for a historic third time after his previous triumphs of 2001 and 2004. After the match he said: "I was a bit nervous because I had the chance to win it three times and did not want to get caught up in the hype, so did not read any papers in the build up. I just wanted to go out there and play my normal game. I knew if the boys went well that I had a chance of winning it. I thought the boys were awesome today. I can sit back now and enjoy it, but I was nervous before the game because everyone was talking about me winning it three times. You have to give credit to the other 16 lads out there because without them I could have won the award and we could not have won the game.

"We had said all week that we had to go out and play as a team, not as individuals. The guys just stuck to the game plan that the gaffer gave us. It was tough, but we came through."

Long was praised by his coach Anderson, who said in his post match press conference: "His kicking was immaculate and for me he has just matured into the role he has been given. He has plenty of sticks in his golf bag. Every now and then I like him to play the two iron but he pulls out the driver on the skinny fairway. But as he has said, he cannot do what he does without the blokes around him and in front of him. When we don't play well it is usually when our big men don't play well either."

Saints' victory was being lapped up by the experienced men in the ranks as much as first time medallists Jamie Lyon, James Roby, James Graham, Jason Cayless, Francis Meli and Maurie Fa'asavalu.

Three times cup medal winner Long said: "This is even better. When I won my first Challenge Cup you think that you are going to win it every week and you don't really take it in. But as you get older you savour it, because this could be my last final. It feels really sweet."

As for his nearest rival in the voting, record breaker Long said: "I thought Wilko was awesome. He pushes up and plays for the team. He is not an individual; he is a grafter who you can always rely on. I knew that if he had stayed on longer he would have probably got the Lance Todd."

True to form Long was destined to write another few headlines before 2006 was out. He was the man handed the skipper's armband when Paul Sculthorpe's season was terminated due another knee injury. As such he was, following another masterful display at the Theatre of Dreams, scene of his match-winning heroics in 1999 and 2002, the man to climb the podium and lift the Super League title.

It had been a long season – too long – and after helping Great Britain beat Australia for the last time despite being left with a bloodied and bandaged face courtesy of a Willie Mason challenge we saw Longy in the news again. He had flown with the rest of the Lions to New Zealand – but a stapled cut eye and dead leg meant he was in no real shape to play – but he did – in the defeat by the Kiwis. And then, with another game and possible final to go, Long dropped the bombshell to coach Brian Noble that he was coming home. He had had a few, mind, but that was not the reason for cutting short his tour and his international career. Although it would be an utter travesty if the events of that last few days of his 2006 season – and the cumulative impact of sleeping pills, red wine and Baileys – devalued his preceding nine months, it nonetheless showed Long as the ultimate enigma. And in the red vee that year he showed leadership and maturity that belied this image of a daft lad from Wigan and he certainly helped turn the class of 2006 into the invincible force it was.

20

September

With the first piece of silverware safely at rest in the Knowsley Road trophy cabinet Saints had a six day turnaround as they fixed their sights firmly on completing the second part of their treble mission when they tackled relegation-threatened Wakefield Trinity.

Although coach Daniel Anderson did not expect his side to be at their physical and mental peak, neither were they going to be in 'Champagne Charlie' mode as they sought the win that would, bar some ridiculous mathematical improbabilities occurring, secure top spot for the second year running.

Post-final celebrations, which traditionally carried on for a few days after the big event, ended the day after Twickenham with the players back in training on Bank Holiday Monday. It was not that Anderson was a real puritanical task master, but with the finishing line so close after a long hard slog he wanted the team to retain their focus. He expected his players to respond for the last six weeks of the season, telling them they could "celebrate as long as they want after October 14 – Grand Final day."

He said: "My aim is to back these boys up on Friday and win the League Leaders' Shield. We can aim for a treble – although this is a little trophy it is still an achievement and a goal that can be rewarded on Friday if we play well.

"I would not expect us to be at our best, physically and mentally, but competitively once we are on the field at Knowsley Road in front of our home fans there is a certain amount of drive. We will prepare professionally and will be better after this game, no matter what happens."

With only three games to play Saints were four points clear of second placed Hull with a much superior points difference. But they were taking nothing for granted and wanted to hit the play-offs with some momentum, probably noting how the Bulls had stampeded their way to Old Trafford the previous year.

Anderson said: "I don't want us to lose another game this year and just because we have won the Challenge Cup does not mean we should have our heads up our own backsides. The desire is to get back into work and achieve more. There is a genuine hunger to defend the League Leaders' Shield and be at Old Trafford. I am very determined to get there."

Saints effectively wrapped up the League Leaders' Shield with a gutsy 34-12 win over the battling Wakefield Trinity Wildcats – an achievement that was largely overlooked by sections of the media, transfixed with the relegation battle.

Although the league table had suggested a straightforward tussle, Wakefield had been a different proposition under coach John Kear and they undoubtedly sensed that Saints might be jaded from their Twickenham endeavours.

They were partly right – with Saints without injured cup winners Willie Talau, Jason Cayless and Jon Wilkin – and they struggled to lift themselves after the emotional highs of the previous week's Challenge Cup Final win. But that only lasted 20 minutes or so, a period which saw the visitors dominate and be rewarded with a six-point lead. But Saints soon overhauled that and showed great resolve in defending their line against some pretty dynamic attack from a robust Trinity team whose members were really battling for their livelihoods.

"It is generally a brutal, confrontational game and if you don't measure up and fight fire with fire you won't compete. That was the good thing, and although it took us 15-20 minutes once we started to confront them I felt very confident," Anderson said.

There was some confrontation, too, with Trinity's Greek international prop Michael Korkidas taking exception to Lyon's lying on, and putting his head into the centre's already bandaged face. The touch judge made what is now a rare foray on to the pitch and Korkidas was red carded. With a numerical advantage Saints eased home with tries from Leon Pryce and a second for wing Ade Gardner wrapping up the points and effectively sealed top spot.

Anderson said: "Wakefield created a number of chances, but our scrambling defence was the best it has been all year. We had situations where their players were getting the ball one or two metres out, with nobody in front of them, but suddenly people were swarming on them. That saved four or five tries."

He was gushing in his praise for Mike Bennett's energetic and enthusiastic display – and what that did for the team – in his first run out in over four months.

"We have a lot of players who have played nearly 30 games this season, but Mike has only played four or five. As a result his energy is lifting players who may be flagging a little bit.

"Added to that he is a very good footballer and a genuine clubman, who is both gritty and selfless in the way he plays. It is great to have him back at this stage in the season. He is one of those players who has missed out on a couple of cup finals, so he is so fired up to participate in the big games. That, in turn, is driving blokes who may have slipped into the relaxed mode otherwise."

The night was not without negatives with prop Nick Fozzard carried off on a stretcher with injuries resembling 'whiplash', but Paul Sculthorpe's precautionary departure, after feeling no power in his leg, caused more concern.

Anderson, however, was focussing on the positives but scratched his head at the apparent underwhelming disregard for the team finishing top of the pile and called for the achievement to be afforded more respect.

He should know – it is often forgotten that Saints had walked away with that particular prize in 2005. But that image of Saints' wounded, bruised and battered class of Super League X was never going to find its way into the hall of fame given the way that year had ended. Maybe those semi-final defeats by Leeds and Bradford should not have diminished the achievement, but there was clearly a feeling that Saints had won nothing.

Most of the blame for that rested with the way the Grand Final concept was rammed down our throats in 1998 when the change from first past the post occurred. It was pretty brutal mechanism adopted to persuade the rugby league public that had been used to, since 1974, the champions being the team finishing top. In 1998, in order to bend attitudes towards one day at Old Trafford being the be all and end all, finishing top was dismissed. Having two competing competitions of value was not considered, maybe because that would have brought question marks over who were the real champions.

Even the late push to awarding a League Leaders' Shield was a belated concession, and one that drew derision with the platter earning the derogatory nickname of the hubcap. Had the authorities rescued the old Championship trophy from the Wigan trophy cabinet and presented that to the team ending the campaign on top would have been a more deserved prize.

However Daniel Anderson, rather than extra trinkets, called for an enhanced cash prize pot to be given to the number one team. He said: "It is very enjoyable to have effectively wrapped up the League Leaders' Shield for the second season running, but that seems to have been quietly received. I believe more value should be placed on finishing first."

"In the NRL there is prize money for coming top of the pile and that gives the achievement an extra level of enhancement. If the competition is going down to the wire I think you would see teams striving even harder for top spot if there was a substantial prize at the end of it. There has been a lot of emphasis placed on the relegation battle this term, but all St Helens can do is carry on playing well. We have set a great standard this year and we aim to carry that form into the play-offs."

The visit of third-placed Leeds, coached by Anderson's former Parramatta colleague Tony Smith, saw the Saints boss in relaxed mood, not simply because his team already had top spot sewn up. He drew confidence from the good football and high level of performance and looked forward to what the Rhinos – potential play-off opponents – would throw at them.

"There is a lot of hunger at training. We are in a good frame of mind. I enjoy the challenge of Leeds because they always rise for us and there is usually only a margin of 6-8 points in it. I want all the challenges that can be given to us before the play-off and if they come here, with their best team, and stick it to us, it will be good," he said.

Leeds did anything but "stick it to them" with stylish Saints wrapping up the second leg of their treble after going through their full repertoire of skills in a ten-try 54-18 triumph, which left the big crowd hollering for an encore.

With the top spot already assured – if not mathematically – the relaxed Saints side let rip, confidently using the full width of the pitch to expose the defensive frailties of a side harbouring Grand Final expectations.

In handing Leeds their heaviest defeat of the season, Saints scored a massive psychological victory and just to throw a barrel of rock salt into those gaping wounds up stepped heavyweight prop Paul Anderson, who neatly stroked the last touchline conversion straight between the uprights to the wild delight of the Popular Side.

The game was as good as over after ten minutes, with Saints crossing for three tries in that spell to leave the visitors shell-shocked. Jamie Lyon showed all of his class to start the ball rolling, taking an inside ball from Keiron Cunningham to cut inside, losing his marker with the subtlest shake of the hips then roaring over. It was the first of his hat-trick which earned him the man of the match award.

Some Saints fans had been almost tormented by Lyon during the course of the two years since he signed from Parramatta via Wee Waa Panthers. Will he come? Will he stay? Will he sign for Wigan? Will he come back after Christmas? Will he re-sign next year?

It was time to stop worrying about hypothetical questions. With Lyon's future sorted at Manly, rugby league fans in the glass town had only a few weeks left to savour the delights of the Australian maestro; an opportunity to simply sit back and marvel at his last few sublimely majestic touches in the red vee. And in subsequent years fans would no doubt pinch themselves and ask if he was really ever here, before giving him the Meninga treatment of 'When is Lyon coming back?'

And as the season reached its peak, Lyon had upped his game a notch and in that game against Leeds he relished the opportunity to handle the ball, possibly as much as he had ever done at Saints. Ade Gardner benefited from that, too, with Lyon providing the assists to his brace of touchdowns.

It was not a one-man show, home-grown heroes Cunningham and Paul Wellens were equally worthy of the man of the match prize with their impeccable stints that night against the Rhinos. The doggedly determined Great Britain full back Wellens sparked the movement that led to Saints' crucial second and third scores from Sean Long and Kiwi wing Francis Meli's 80 metre rumble up the touchline. There was no way back for Leeds after that – and the game was already well won when Wellens grabbed two tries in three minutes. After all that quality rugby – there is one particular segment of play that most Saints fans there that night will still recall some years on. Paul Anderson's touchline conversion provided a real coup de grace for the ailing Rhinos.

Anderson said: "I didn't look at Baloo as much as I looked at the Popular Side and they went absolutely bananas. A lot of people got a lot of enjoyment from that kick. When players finish their career – they invariably sneak in a shot at goal."

But picking the bones through the performance and the celebrations, the coach added: "We got off to a blistering start with three tries in the opening ten minutes, which more or less wrapped it up. It was a thoroughly enjoyable day and the celebration in the end was a reflection of what our squad has achieved this year. We spoke about winning the League Leaders' Shield and they were commended for it in the dressing room afterwards.

"It was Longy's birthday celebration and James Graham's 21st so there was genuinely a lot of emotion around the day and they celebrated."

Again, Anderson urged caution, for despite being eight points ahead of their nearest opponents Hull – the big prize was an entirely different proposition. However, Saints were in much better physical shape – and the leadership of the group was spread wider too.

"We will knuckle down because we all know we won the shield last year then failed to make the Grand Final. There was a marked difference in the atmosphere from the same presentation last term – we won Saturday's game for a start. This year we are healthier and added to that our young players Roby, Wilkin, Gardner, Graham and Fa'asavalu are all more mature and better.

"They may be better, but it is still our key personnel who are firing. Leon, Longy, Wello and Keiron are all playing well – and they are the spine of the team."

So with the League Leaders' Shield in the cabinet, Saints had every excuse to stick their cue in the rack for a week, put their feet up and keep their powder dry for the play-offs. Not a chance. They were, after all, playing neighbours and big-spending wannabes Warrington. The Wolves desperately wanted to be up there winning silverware – but back in 2006 they would have settled for a win against the Saints.

They had just one summer era triumph against the Saints – that a hollow one against 12-men in the week before the 2001 Challenge Cup Final. Anderson knew all about that history, that back then, was always the pre-match talking point.

He said: "I am certainly wary of their abilities and of their desires to play well against St Helens and they will be looking to peak in the play-offs. They are improving, but we are not going to give them a leg up this weekend."

Warrington fancied it and their dislike was palpable. They more or less said as much by playing a far from neighbourly Kaiser Chiefs number 'Every day I love you less and less!' as the Saints ran on to the field. And at the end of the 80 minutes, they gave the Wolves fans new reasons to curse and go home to stick pins in their red and white voodoo dolls.

The Wires had stormed into a 16-point lead after just 13 minutes to whip up three-quarters of a raucous sell-out crowd into a near frenzy. Warrington looked to be on the verge of claiming only their second win in 29 Super League era encounters – but then Saints switched themselves on and the Wires blew a fuse.

It turned out that Saints had been just like a cat, toying playfully with a mouse before nonchalantly snapping its head off, rattling in 28 unanswered points. Although it was hardly vintage stuff from Saints, who had been struggling with flu all week, once they got their noses in front they never looked like losing.

Wolves started like a house on fire, and Lee Briers pushed his side around the pitch with his skilful boot but it is unlikely he would have got the same time on the ball had Jason Hooper been playing. A Jon Wilkin try was just the warm-up – with four tries in the 14 minutes – braces for Ade Gardner and Paul Wellens – before the break giving Saints a 12 point lead to the delight of those travelling fans packed into the West Stand, who rejoiced, chanting "We gave you 16 start!"

Saints eased up in the second half, which let Warrington back in and had the unfortunate by-product of provoking the Wolves drummer to create a cacophony that bordered on noise pollution. Saints still had enough to wrap it up 38-30 and finish the year a remarkable eight points clear of runners-up Hull FC.

Top of the pile for the second year running, Saints were in an altogether much better shape to get through to Old Trafford than they were the year before. In front of them for their first bite of the cherry was Hull FC, a team that had shown some steely resolve since the appointment of Peter Sharp.

Under the top six system both the top two teams had sat out the first weekend of combat, observing as reigning champions Bradford steamrollered Salford while Warrington produced their first ever play-off win to eliminate the previous year's runners-up Leeds.

With Leeds going out, and Wigan again failing to make qualification – the least of their worries that season – the chance of a team outside of the quartet that had been the original big four making the final was high. Nobody was ruling out the Bulls, who had a taste for the Theatre of Dreams having made six of the previous eight Grand Finals.

Saints were in good shape, but in the week building up to the semi, skipper Paul Sculthorpe was ruled out for the remaining games of the season after it was decided that his troublesome knee injury needed an operation. Bizarre as it sounds, Saints had got used to playing without the two-time Man of Steel winner. But the news was less palatable for the man himself, who had been hoping to delay the operation and was understandably keen to skipper the side at Old Trafford.

The Sculthorpe blow was softened because Saints had plenty of cover in the back row, particularly with Mike Bennett returning to the fold and Great Britain squad players Lee Gilmour and Jon Wilkin in fine form.

Anderson said: "If our last encounter here at Knowsley Road is anything to go by, when they just pipped us by a point, it should be a cracking game. We both know each other's qualities and know what both sides can offer. It is about what can be actioned on the field now. It is going to be a tight game, but they will be thoroughly prepared and we won't be underestimating them.

"With the media fixation with the relegation issue Hull have slipped under the radar a little this year but they have done well to finish the season in second spot.

"Hooker Richard Swain controls a lot of Hull's direction and scrum half Richard Horne is a very underrated, but very good player. Paul Cooke, too, is obviously a very talented ball player, but they have a real tradesman-like team. They have genuinely honest rugby league players and have a very strong pack."

The game did throw up one immediate duel – after the Great Britain selectors had opted to take Hull's Gareth Raynor ahead of Ade Gardner for autumn's Tri-Nations tour to Australia and New Zealand.

Anderson, as an ex-Test coach of New Zealand, did not wish to intrude on to the minefield of another coach's selection dilemmas. But he did say: "Ade will be very disappointed to miss out on selection for the Great Britain Tri-Series squad and I don't doubt that he will be out to show again on Friday that he still a genuine candidate in the future.

"I don't think there is much between all of the wingers selected for Great Britain. I am disappointed for Ade and think he would have been perfectly suited for Tri-Series rugby because he is a big winger and his speed and power is an advantage."

Speaking ahead of the semi, Wellens said: "We expect a very committed Hull team to come here. They are a very workmanlike side and consistent, which shows in where they finished in the table. They are also very thorough in their preparation and are a team that don't give a lot away, a feature that is ideally suited for play-off football."

There was not a great deal in it in the end in what was a gripping contest, with the 12-8 margin coming courtesy of a crucial try from Francis Meli. The big wing had to reach down to his bootstraps to take the crucial pass before stumbling over the line, clinching a passage to Saints' first Grand Final since 2002.

The crucial touchdown came on the hour mark courtesy of a dynamic Sean Long break, backed by Lee Gilmour, and broke the deadlock just as it looked set to go into drop goal time. Despite that try, Jamie Lyon's failure with the touchline conversion meant neither Saints nor their fanatical fans could breathe any easier for the remaining nerve-jangling 20 minutes.

It was, however, a cracking collision between the top two sides who had arguably been head and shoulders above the rest of Super League XI. Although there were few points, it was an utterly compelling, nail biting contest, which had the raucous 14,000 plus crowd transfixed. Hull came into the game as the only side to have lowered Saints' colours at Knowsley Road this term – and their formula was the same.

There is nothing particularly fancy about their game plan, they simply tried to wear Saints down with a combination of their heavy duty, workmanlike pack and the kicking game of Paul Cooke, who constantly drilled the ball downfield and hoped for an error. But Saints' back three of Paul Wellens, Francis Meli and Ade Gardner were equal to that task, defusing those kicks to both neutralise the threat and then create a solid platform to launch the counter attack.

With both defences soaking up all that was thrown at them with some ferocious tackling on show, aided by a pretty stingy 10 metres served up by referee Ashley Klein, it took something of a freak score to break the deadlock on 17 minutes when Wellens flashed a hurried pass away from dummy half, which flapped backwards off intended target Gilmour and was fly hacked on by Lyon. Gardner nipped in to collect, leaving Hull defenders Kirk Yeaman and Gareth Raynor flat footed en route to the line. The video ref gave Saints the thumbs up, and Lyon chipped in with the extras.

But eight minutes later Hull hit back with a classy try which saw the impressive Cooke feature twice and a number of players running good angles before Great Britain squad man Kirk Yeaman polished it off in the corner.

Cooke and Lyon exchanged penalties but Saints' pack, in which Keiron Cunningham, Paul Anderson and Jason Cayless were dominant, began to win the war of attrition in the middle. But the dashing performance of James Roby, whose extra yard of pace and variety caught out the Humbersiders' defence and stole those extra few metres, was instrumental in tipping the balance of power Saints way leading to Meli's match winner.

In the weeks building up to that game news had begun to filter out about the plight of former Saints and Hull full back Steve Prescott, who had been diagnosed with cancer and given barely a few months to live.

The bucket collectors at Knowsley Road that night were overwhelmed with donations and there was an outpouring of sympathy and support for the likeable number one. As a gesture of solidarity, Hull FC came out on Grand Final night wearing Prescott 1 tracksuits.

Of course, those few months became seven years as Steve fought pseudomyxoma peritonei – a rare cancer of the abdomen – with every fibre of his being.

It soon became pretty clear that it was not sympathy that Steve wanted – in a super human effort he took on a series of gruelling challenges to raise awareness of his disease, funds for The Christie Hospital and Try Assist and demonstrate that there is always hope, no matter what the odds.

Sadly, Steve died in November 2013 after complications following a multiple organ transplant that had rid him of the cancer – but this extraordinary man has left a lasting legacy in his home town, across the rugby league community and beyond.

21

Ade Gardner – the Try Machine

Saints wing Ade Gardner played some of the best rugby of his career in 2006 with his link up with Jamie Lyon propelling him up the scoring charts. One of his most crucial scores was the one that broke the deadlock in the play-off semi-final win against Hull – one that settled a few butterflies. It was a compelling tussle in front of a big noisy crowd. And aside from the glittering prize of a place at the Grand Final at stake, Gardner had the side-issue of his personal duel with Gareth Raynor to consider.

Gardner explained: "I was really nervous going into it because we had lost the semi-final the year before to Leeds after coming top and ended up not making it to Old Trafford. The Hull game was similar conditions, too, to that game and was quite a drizzly night.

"I was nervous going in – that happens when you have been the more successful team because there is a bit more pressure on you. It started a bit up and down for us and then I got the first score from something out of nothing."

Saints did not stay in front for long with Kirk Yeaman scoring to delight the large travelling black and white hordes, something that Gardner said reminded them that it was still going to be a long night at the office, and maybe temporarily opened a few doubts after what had happened earlier in the campaign.

"After Yeaman scored it really dawned on us that it was going to be a tough game. They had already beaten us once that year with a drop goal at Knowsley Road and then they led with a penalty just after the break. The second half was a case of all hands to the pump – I remember taking a big high crossfield kick to the corner. Wello was getting hammered with high balls because Paul Cooke was on fire and so too were Hull FC.

"There was real relief afterwards because we knew Hull were a tough side. After the game we went for a beer and there was real relief because we had played really well and were going to Old Trafford."

Gardner had plenty to fire him up for a big performance, since learning five days previously that despite his fine form and scoring prowess he had lost the Great Britain shirt that he had worn proudly a couple of months earlier at Knowsley Road.

As fate would have it, he was up against the man he had lost it to in that semi.

Gardner recalls: "Playing opposite Gareth Raynor was quite a big motivation for me. The Sunday before the game Great Britain coach Brian Noble had rung me up to tell me I was not going on the Tri-Nations tour.

"I was really, really annoyed by it. It was a big motivation to finish the year on a high. To be honest I had taken it for a granted because I had played for Great Britain earlier in the year in the one-off Test against the Kiwis. I was the top try scorer in the competition and playing the best rugby of my career so not getting picked baffled me. It was not really Gaz I had a beef with, it was some of the other boys he took instead that I had an issue with. Still from a Saints point of view it gave me major motivation because I really wanted to go on that tour and it would have really capped my season off but it was not to be."

Gardner had enjoyed a great season, one in which the hands on coaching from Daniel Anderson and Alan Wilson had benefited him as much as being switched to play outside Jamie Lyon.

Darren Albert had left to join Cronulla at the end of 2005 and was replaced by Francis Meli, but Anderson threw the opportunity to the 22-year-old Barrovian.

"It was really exciting for me. At the end of the previous season Daniel had pulled me to one side and told me that I was going to be playing outside Jamie Lyon in 2006. I had played pretty much most of my time at Saints outside Willie Talau on the left – but I saw playing outside Jamie as a big opportunity for me. That is no disrespect to Willie, but on the left we were the grafters of the team, doing a lot of the work and carries from dummy half, whereas Jamie and Darren were getting the tries.

"I saw it as a good opportunity for me to get a bagful of tries when Darren left. We did not know how we were going to fit in and how we were going to gel as a team," Gardner declared.

The match-up worked, but it would be disrespectful to class the set-up as similar to the partnership between Mal Meninga and little known winger Sean Day, who had one glorious season in 1984/85 playing outside the Australian legend. Gardner had a much better toolkit in his locker and he worked hard on his game – it was not a case of it all being put on a plate for him by Lyon. Many of his tries that term were a product of his ability to attack the high kicks of Sean Long. It was a big feature of that year – and why not with two big wingers and a scrum half that could put it on a sixpence.

Gardner explained: "That was the first season where we started doing kicks to corners. When we went to Torremelinos for pre-season camp, and we were there for about a week, our back three hammered attacking the high ball. It was something we had never really done too much of in previous years. In the game as a whole it was still a relatively new ploy that not many teams were using. We had kicked a few times for Albi in 2005 and he had scored a couple of times here and there. That was a big focus for us in pre-season as outside backs."

A lot of hard work gets done in pre-season, work on core-skills, strength work and getting the things right that often get sidelined once the first ball of the season is kicked and all training becomes match specific. Gardner gained a lot from the fresh pairs of eyes that were looking at his game and using his height and athleticism to optimum benefit.

"It was Daniel's first off season with us and he brought Alan Wilson on board as technical adviser. I recall pre-season being really technical and going according to plan, so I felt quite confident going into the season that we were going to be one of the better teams," he said.

"I have always had really good jumping ability but Daniel was brilliant at explaining things to me like a school teacher. To get it

165

across to me he said he would teach me the mechanics of doing it and the more I did it, the better I would get.

"Even on the captain's run the day before a game we would literally be learning how to jump as high as possible, often they were just small kicks but the idea was to learn how to jump and catch a ball at its highest point. We would literally hammer it the whole time. I was slowly getting there and getting the process and getting better in training, but it wasn't until we played Hull away when I outjumped Gareth Raynor that it clicked.

"As soon as I got one then I scored another ten from kicks to corner. Until you get confidence to do it in a game you don't link it all up in a positive way in your mind. Daniel was very good at that – at teaching the little bits of one particular skill and going through the process of getting better at it. After I got that one I could not wait to get even more. On play five if we were ever stuck for an option he would put it up in the air and give me a chance to get it. That was a really big thing for me and that side of my game really pushed my career. It took off from that point onwards. Pat Richards had come in at Wigan and he was doing it, but there were not many other wingers doing it – and with being 6ft 2in that set me apart."

Anderson had clearly identified using Gardner's height and athleticism. He said: "Ade had never caught as many balls from kicks for tries as he did that year – with 11 in total compared to only one that year. It is down to his hard work and learning what his body can do."

It was not all about scoring tries, the right hand gang had plenty of work to do in defence but the opposition got little change out of the Long, Lyon and Gardner trio.

Gardner said: "Right edge is the toughest side to defend in rugby league so teams stack up their best players on that side because it is usually people's favourite passing side. It is difficult to play on the right wing – we had Longy defending inside us as well and he was a good defender, but as a small bloke and key player they were going to throw a lot of traffic down his side – and they did.

"We had to be on our mettle because we had a lot of traffic. The big thing about Daniel is that he shored up our defence massively and there was a noticeable change. They were not big changes – it was more of a defensive philosophy and he went through things that would make us efficient in defending.

"These were just little things that we would drill. We were never bored in training but Daniel would literally drill in those fundamentals of rugby that would make you a better player so when you went out on the park you did it automatically because we were doing it the whole time."

Gardner played a different style of game that year than he did in subsequent seasons and on numerous occasions he would take the man on the outside. He said: "It was great. We played with a smile on our faces. And as for the sight of me running down the flank, instead of cutting inside, well that was just the nature of the game then. Our forwards and men inside me were good at creating space, I was presented with a lot more opportunities. In the years that followed the dynamics of the game changed a bit, and my game has changed with it. I feel a bit like a front rower now.

"I played every game that year apart from two Catalan aways because my little boy was born on Easter Monday so I missed the first one, and then they sent a young side for the second one. It was one of the best years of my life – we won everything and our Zak was born on 18 April. It was a really good year, that."

22

Theatre of Dreams

Saints enjoyed their tour of the Old Trafford Theatre of Dreams on the Monday before the final. The first timers in particular really soaked it up, walking around, not on, the hallowed turf and posing for pictures in the dressing rooms beneath the pictures of the Manchester United stars.

As is the norm a group of around six or seven players was despatched to the press conference to help promote the game. Pre-Old Trafford press conferences invariably take the same formula which must frustrate the life out of the combatants. They start out with a top table, in this case Daniel Anderson and Peter Sharp, sitting up there between the Super League trophy with the sponsors logo in the backdrop. There are few questions because every journalist present wants to get a 'one-to-one', and then there is a mad scramble to collar players and coaches.

Some players will be in bigger demand than others, with the nationals needing a 'story' interview and therefore leaving some on the side checking their phones and uncomfortably left on the edge of the room like someone waiting to be asked for a dance at a school disco.

This experience was first time around for Jamie Lyon, who wandered away in disbelief after one interview muttering: "That's the seventh time I have answered the exact same questions!"

The Saints players were always very good and professional – publicity generates ticket sales and attracts sponsors and pays wages. They invariably play the game at events like this. Speaking before he was collared by a waiting queue of a dozen reporters, Daniel Anderson spelled out what he was looking forward to: "The Grand Final at Old Trafford is going to be a massive occasion in front of a packed house and we all know that we are playing for a very special trophy. We have had our stadium walkabout and although I have been here before to watch a couple of games, this is my first taste of Old Trafford as a combatant. It is a magnificent stadium. There is a good feeling in the camp as we build up to Saturday. We are not cocky, but we can certainly be confident and know where we want to go as a team.

"Hull are a very good side and everyone knows that we have been the most consistent two teams in the competition this year. There has been nothing between Saints and Hull this year and both teams know that, so this is a fair representation of a Grand Final.

"In the previous game we did not have great ball control, but we had magnificent defence and that is what won us the game. I think we need to play better than that to win. Although we go into the game as favourites – as we have done in all 35 games this season – that does not faze us. We respect what we have done this year and that is why we have that favourites tag. Having already won the Challenge Cup and the League Leaders' Shield, it would be very special to win all trophies in the same season.

"It would perhaps be a fitting reward as this team has provided countless moments of enjoyment for both Saints fans and rugby league supporters generally. Although we have played very well this year, nothing we have done so far this season counts towards the Grand Final, even though in our own mindset it helps to confirm what we can do. We are facing an opposition who are arguably the toughest team to break down."

The Grand Final would be one packed with emotion, not least because two of the central planks of the team for the past two years were leaving. "It promises to be an emotional night with the departure of Paul Anderson and Jamie Lyon after two tremendous seasons at Knowsley Road. But those emotions will have to be kept in check, particularly leading up to the game. It is Baloo's last ever game as a player and Jamie's final one in a red vee before he goes back to Australia. I am lucky that Jamie has been in a Grand Final with Parramatta in the NRL and Baloo has been in five with Bradford, so they both know the pressures along with our other experienced players."

For good or ill Old Trafford would become a regular haunt of the Saints in the last half of the noughties, but back in 2006 it was first time around for quite a few members of the squad. Saints had not run out at the Theatre of Dreams since 2002, that most gripping of finales sealed by Sean Long's masterfully executed drop goal.

In fact, prior to the '06 showpiece that memorable match had been the last time James Roby had set foot in Old Trafford as a 16-year-old spectator bouncing up and down with delight in the Saints end after that last gasp win over a Bradford team then featuring latter day Saints Paul Anderson, Lee Gilmour and Leon Pryce.

Fast forward four years and Roby was transformed from a young supporter from Blackbrook into a terrace favourite with his own song, with his impact off the bench being a key aspect of Saints' play this term. And two weeks before the final Roby underlined his growing reputation by claiming the man of the match award in Saints' tense triumph over Hull to book their place at the Theatre of Dreams. That stadium nickname was such an appropriate description for the former Blackbrook Royal, who enjoyed a season beyond his wildest dreams in 2006.

Speaking in the run up to the game, Roby said: "As a kid you dream of representing Great Britain, winning a Challenge Cup Final and playing in a Grand Final and I have done that all at once. It is like going on a rollercoaster ride really. I really never expected to be in this position before my 21st birthday.

"Apart from the winning, it is just a great honour to play in the side. We have a really good blend – and on and off the field we are really good mates. I am just excited about playing – I am not nervous, just ready to go and can't wait for Saturday to get out there."

Roby's deceptive strength, eye for a gap and blistering pace from dummy half caused consternation among even the toughest defences, and that was shown when Hull could not put him down in the semi-final. But he knew he was going to have to do it all again in the big one.

He said: "Hull always seem to hit a patch of form when they come up against us and always play well. They gave us a hard game the other week and that took a lot out of us defensively. But they have had to back up with a tough game against Bradford last week and hopefully that will work in our favour.

"We know it is going to be a massive battle on the pitch and hopefully we can come out on top. So far we have won everything on offer. Our defence has given us the edge this year. Since Daniel has arrived our defence has improved dramatically and that is a credit to his policy."

Full back Paul Wellens, who back then was a veteran of three Grand Finals was hoping some of that big match experience would rub off on the many Old Trafford debutants in Saints' ranks. Indeed, he knew exactly how those younger players were feeling given he was just a teenager when he was thrown into Ellery Hanley's title-winning squad in 1999.

Again, speaking in the build up to that week, Wellens recalled: "I was 19 when I came off the bench for the last 25 minutes against Bradford. In that match we had to do some tigerish defending but we managed to hang on. It was a fantastic day to enjoy at such a young age, but that just whetted my appetite to have another taste."

He did that, and has encountered the brutal realities of the blood and thunder occasion. In what was Saints' previous appearance at Old Trafford Wellens bravely went down to field a loose ball, only to cop a stray boot from Bulls centre Brandon Costin and was immediately led off the field with a fractured cheekbone and spent the rest of the game under observation in the changing room.

"My face was in a pretty bad way, but I was made up that we won. It was quite a weird feeling though obviously I would not want to go through that again. It is fantastic to be back here. We also have a few young lads who have never been involved in this situation and it was great to see their excitement. I am just hoping we can remain focused and continue to do what we have been doing all year and put the icing on the cake of a fantastic season," Wellens said.

But he knew there was hard work to be done, if the semi-final and previous home league game was anything to go by. Wellens had seen at close quarters how the Black and Whites had become a different team under Peter Sharp.

"The last one was as tough a game as you could play in – very physical and one of those where neither team was giving much away. Every little inch on the field was fought for and I expect this Saturday to be the same. Hull are a very workmanlike side and get about their business well, so we are going to have to be at our absolute best. Under Peter Sharp they have taken their game to another level, as was shown by their winning streak. We fully respect Hull, but it is about doing our own job and coming up with the performance," he said.

23

Grand Final – Mission Accomplished

The Super League XI Grand Final was arguably the noisiest we had known, it was certainly the biggest gate with a sell-out crowd of 72,575 watching events unfold.

What they saw was Daniel Anderson's class of 2006 stake their claim as the best-ever Saints side after completing the domestic treble in such emphatic style at a raucous Old Trafford. It was a big claim to make and only history will judge whether townsfolk will be talking about the sublime passing skills of Jamie Lyon, the guile of Sean Long and the doggedness of Paul Wellens in 40 years' time in the revered way Tom van Vollenhoven, Cliff Watson and Alex Murphy are still discussed.

But what was not in dispute was that this set of Knowsley Roaders had been head and shoulders above the rest of Super League XI, lifting all three cups and losing just four games during a long, gruelling season. It was not hard to point out where this side had had such a decisive, clinical edge – defence – and that was another key feature of the Grand Final win.

Saints' sides have traditionally never been short on attacking flair, but in the 2006 season that trait was complemented by a formidable defensive effort and a level of consistency not seen at Knowsley Road since Shaun McRae's double-winning side of 1996. No player epitomised that body-on-the-line commitment more than Man of Steel Paul Wellens, who capped a fine individual week with a string of last-ditch tackles earning him the Harry Sunderland award for the player of the match.

There were other candidates in support, with stand-in skipper

Sean Long pulling Saints' strings with a magnificent kicking game that led directly to two of their five tries. And up front, every single forward did his duty to subdue an industrious Hull pack that had bested them at Knowsley Road back in June.

Hull, backed by a big section of the crowd, tore into action from the first whistle and only a timely fingertip touch from Paul Anderson, in his swansong appearance, stopped Shane McMenemy from taking the scoring pass.

With Hull's halves Richard Horne and Paul Cooke kicking smartly, Saints' back three had to be on their mettle with Francis Meli just managing to nudge one such kick dead. However, the Humbersiders had the bit between their teeth and only a last-gasp double tackle from Jamie Lyon and Wellens foiled Gareth Raynor at the corner flag.

Having withstood that early pressure, Saints turned defence into attack and with virtually their first opportunity Meli caught Long's pinpoint kick to touch down.

Hull, though, showed why they have been up there as Saints' biggest rivals this term and again Cooke had a key role. The lanky stand-off's kick wide was left by Meli, allowing Motu Tony and McMenemy to combine to send Sid Domic over.

At 4-4, it turned into an arm wrestle, with Saints marginally on top thanks to some potent attacking play from Lee Gilmour on the right. Twice the supporting Lyon, playing his last game in the red vee, looked to fashion an opening for wing partner Ade Gardner. Unfortunately, on the first occasion the Aussie's blind pass went wide just as the winger had cut inside. And then two minutes later Hull full back Shaun Briscoe nailed Gardner with a crash tackle that bundled the Saints man into touch.

Then Saints did what the great Wigan side of the late 1980s always seemed to do and hit their opponents with a sucker punch just before the break. Hull were in a fine attacking position when they were penalised for crossing, to the disgust of coach Sharp who waved his arms around with rage in the stands. Saints immediately took play to the opposite end with long-striding Leon Pryce storming through a feeble tackle and then darting past Briscoe on a diagonal burst to the line. Lyon's touchline conversion gave Saints a six-point cushion going into the break.

Saints then took the game by the scruff of the neck with two tries in a four-minute spell after the restart. Willie Talau's try came from some quick thinking when Keiron Cunningham's untidy pass missed James Graham, allowing James Roby to clean up and toss an overhead pass to Hooper. The energetic loose forward looped his arms over the tackler to send Talau steaming in for a converted score.

Then Gardner, who was by this stage winning his duel with the man who took his Great Britain jersey from him, out-jumped Raynor to Long's high ball and just about got it under control before grounding. Another magnificent goal from Lyon made it a 16-point advantage.

But despite that lead Saints were taking no chances and their defence remained as stingy as ever, with Wellens hauling down Richard Horne in front of the sticks and in the next play covering across to the corner flag to wrestle Tony into touch. It was Hull's last big effort to get back into the game, but that ended when Meli foiled another attack by covering back to nudge Lee Radford's grubber dead before Tony could get his hands to it.

As they had done so ruthlessly in the first half, Saints turned defence into attack with Talau's big hit on Briscoe dislodging the ball. Moments later and a barnstorming run from Maurie Fa'asavalu was halted on the line, only for the big Samoan to flick a pass out of the back door to send Cunningham over to conclude the scoring.

And the defensive spirit that Saints had shown since week one of the season was epitomised by the way Wellens bravely dived upon Yeaman's kick like a soccer goalkeeper. Braver still given that this was virtually in the same spot where the full-back's cheekbone was smashed into something resembling a box of cornflakes barely two minutes into his previous Grand Final appearance. That was not something that had played on the local hero's mind and he gave a near faultless 80-minute display to walk away with the man of the match.

Wellens underlined just why he was named Super League's Man of Steel with an inspirational defensive performance that earned him the Grand Final man of the match award. The locally-born full back has epitomised the defensive resolve that has underpinned Saints treble success this campaign.

And the rock at the back again led by example, making try-saving tackles across the 80 minutes to repel Hull's efforts.

In the seventh minute Wello combined with Jamie Lyon to hurtle across to the corner and force Hull winger Gareth Raynor into touch.

But it was in the 56th minute that the Saints number one excelled himself with full back defensive play of the highest order that possibly clinched the Harry Sunderland Trophy.

As Lee Radford broke clear with Richard Horne on his shoulder, the Hull forward appeared set to draw Saints' last line of defence. But Wellens, realising a team-mate was covering Radford, intelligently backed away from the ball-carrier. Radford was forced to make the pass to Horne but because the Saints full back had not committed himself he was able to swiftly cover the ground and tackle the scrum half.

From the next play-the-ball Hull shipped the ball right to Motu Tony but remarkably Wellens had covered the ground and was in position to haul the winger down. From that moment Hull's resistance appeared to wilt and even when Horne again broke through in the 69th minute Saints 'Mr Consistency' was there to deny him.

Afterwards, the 26-year-old was typically modest about his achievements, saying: "The Harry Sunderland Trophy stands right up there with all the other trophies. Some great players have won this award. I think it is steeped in history and I'm grateful for receiving it. It would be unfair for me to receive awards like this without mentioning fantastic team-mates and coaching staff.

"It's very easy to receive the pats on the back but I play in a great side with some great players and I'm thoroughly grateful for the position I am in."

The Super League Trophy was proudly lifted aloft by skipper Sean Long, who said Saints had overcome the weight of expectation to clinch the victory. They had gone into the final as odds-on favourites and the scrum half said in the post match conference: "There was a lot of pressure on our side – we were favourites and the pressure was on us to deliver. But I thought the boys rose to the occasion and rose to another level and full credit to them. It was a great performance and I thought it was the best performance in a Grand Final by us."

That was praise indeed given Long had been central to two nerve-wracking crackers against Bradford and a derby final win over Wigan in 2000.

Long, who claimed his fourth and final Grand Final winner's ring, was instrumental in the victory, creating tries in either half for wingers Francis Meli and Ade Gardner through superbly-positioned cross-field kicks.

But it was the Saints captain's tactical kicking game which pushed the opponents' back three into the corners of the Old Trafford pitch that Hull coach Peter Sharp thought was crucial.

Asked how good this treble-winning Saints side was, Long said that history would judge them. "I have been here ten years and this is the best team I've been involved with. It's just the strength in depth, the bench we have and the fact we even had to leave out two internationals. Who knows, maybe in 20 or 30 years time we will look back and say maybe we were a great side," he said.

Coach Daniel Anderson paid tribute to Grand Final man-of-the match Paul Wellens, but also had words of praise for the two other pillars of the side, Long and Cunningham.

Anderson said: "Wello has been a magnificent anchor for our team and the cornerstone of how we have built. I think Keiron, Longy and Wello have been the spine of my team since I arrived and have been superb. To have those three players – which I think are the best in their position in this country is an absolute privilege."

Afterwards Hull boss Sharp agreed: "The game went away from us a minute before half-time – we made a mistake with the football and then compounded that by letting a try in."

He added though that Saints were worthy winners: "St Helens were great – they defended magnificently well. St Helens are a very good side – and definitely the best side here in the UK."

Daniel Anderson took a few days to soak it in before penning his column for the *St Helens Star*. He wrote: "Winning the Super League title, the League Leaders' Shield and Challenge Cup in the one season is a tremendous achievement.

"The Grand Final was a very special occasion and a fantastic event to have been part of. In defeating Hull we played to the level that we have done in all the big games this season. It was a performance that underlined we are the best team in the competition and once again we defended magnificently. There were a number of enormous plays – tackles that saved tries – but also some brutal defence.

"Wello stands out for the three or four tackles he made to prevent tries, but there was also crucial cover tackles by Jamie Lyon and Jon Wilkin in the first half.

"And, prior to Keiron Cunningham's second-half try, Willie Talau absolutely belted a Hull player to win us possession. Since the victory there has been a lot said about where this treble places the current Saints side in history. I think history will judge this side as one of very high-quality that was capable of absorbing any pressure thrown at them.

"From my point of view, I'm just delighted to be part of the winning team and winning club that Saints is, although I must admit three days on from the final and I'm feeling the wear-and-tear of a long season somewhat."

For the record the Grand Final teams were:

Saints – Wellens; Gardner, Lyon, Talau, Meli; Pryce, Long; P. Anderson, Cunningham, Cayless, Gilmour, Wilkin, Hooper. Subs: Roby, Graham, Fa'asavalu, Bennett.

Hull – Briscoe; Tony, Domic, Yeaman, Raynor; Cooke, R. Horne; Dowes, Swain, Carvell, McMenemy, Radford, Washbrook. Subs: Whiting, G. Horne, Wheeldon, King.

24

Paul Wellens' Grand Final

The deafening noise. That was the first thing that Saints full back Paul Wellens noticed when the teams walked out to the centre of Old Trafford. And to show how meticulous Saints' preparation had been for the game they had actually trained in the noise ahead of the Hull showdown. Not that anything could simulate the cacophony of noise from the voices and air-horns of 73,000 people.

It was not just the noise, it was nerves that both teams had to handle. Having been front runners from week two, Saints had most at stake and much, much more to lose. They had the favourites tag but with it came massive expectation. Looking down the respective teamsheets, Saints had so many more men who had been in this pressure cooker environment before that you would expect them to handle it better.

The Hull encounter was Paul Wellens' fourth Grand Final – although his previous one had been ended prematurely when Brandon Costin's boot smashed his cheekbone – and that experience was one factor in producing an exemplary performance that saw him add the Harry Sunderland Award to the Man of Steel honour he had won earlier in the week building up to the game.

Wellens said: "There was pressure, huge pressure because we were the stand-out team throughout the season. Although there was pressure there was never any panic. We were confident and self-assured and knew if we went and did what we needed to do we would win the game. Obviously we knew that there were going to be periods in the game that would be tough and we had to defend our line, but we had shown in the past we could do that. We had a lot of experience in the team; people who knew how to handle the emotion of a big occasion. Jamie Lyon had played in Test matches and of course – we had the Challenge Cup experience a few weeks previously and that helped.

"It was so noisy with all the horns going on – but once the game goes on you shut it out. It is something we mentioned in the week building up – as such we trained at Knowsley Road ahead of the game with speakers on, playing music full belt, just to get used to it. It is all good in training because there is nobody there and so you can hear all the calls for moves. It also got to the point where we were telepathic because we were doing the simple plays all the time. It was not so much we needed to hear the call, but if Sean Long went there, Leon knew where he had to move to and then likewise myself. It became fluent."

Saints were exceedingly well equipped to deal with the pressure and Hull – a cursory glance down the teamsheet, particular the calibre of player they could throw off the interchange bench, instilled in them a sense of belief that over the 80 minutes they would have the tools to do the job, even if that meant being patient.

Wellens added: "We knew that with the bench we had no need to panic in a match. We would look at other teams' starting 13s and then match it, but our bench improved our team where in most cases teams were weakened by subs. In Maurie, Robes and Jammer, and during the course of the season sometimes Vinnie, sometimes Fozz, we knew that our bench would not only not let us down but they would take us to another level. We knew being patient was not a bad thing because Hull would get tired tackling these blokes constantly.

"Our props – it was like a bowling attack – one that could bowl on a damp wicket, one in the dry and another when the batsmen were tired. I know Jason Cayless struggled with injuries in subsequent seasons – but that year he was phenomenal. Paul Anderson had great hands and could pass like a half back. He could hit Long on the button every time with a pass. James Graham brings what he brings and Maurie Fa'asavalu was a wrecking ball.

"Keiron would get his foot in the door and Robes would kick it through. On the left Francis Meli and Willie Talau was the Islander combination, which worked really well, on the right Jamie and Ade struck up a real rapport. It seemed wherever we looked on the field there were teams within teams and they all knew what they were doing. That comes down to smart coaching and identifying who works best with who. It worked for us."

Hull broke new ground in getting to Old Trafford – all the previous finals had involved finalists drawn exclusively from the big four club of Saints, Wigan, Leeds and Bradford. They meant business that year and were one of only four teams to beat Saints in 2006.

They also threw everything at Saints in the play-off game at Knowsley Road, one that only tipped the way of the homesters courtesy of a late Francis Meli try. It meant that whatever the bookmakers' odds, the Black and Whites were turning up to give it to Saints.

"The Hull semi was, in some respects, tougher than the Grand Final. It could have gone either way and was a wet night. In games like that you talk about Daniel Anderson's influence – in years previously if we had only scored 12 points in a semi-final you would probably think we would have lost. But we knew that we were as good defensively as we were offensively.

"The Grand Final was tough – even with 20 minutes to go Hull kept coming at us and we had to defend, defend and defend our line. Even though we won 26-4 it always came back to our defence and the work Daniel had done there.

"We knew within our group that if we only conceded a few points then we were going to win."

Hull had plenty of craft in their team and Saints had learned to their cost how effective, if a little old school and unorthodox, the lanky loose forward cum stand off Paul Cooke could be. But ex-schoolmaster Daniel Anderson was good at learning lessons and adopting tactics to neutralise danger. In Cooke's case the antidote was probably 90 per cent Jason Hooper.

Wellens explained: "People look at kickers and defenders but it is a team responsibility – a job for 13 players. So if the ball goes up and if you can buy your catcher one second it could make all the difference. Jason Hooper was good at kick pressure – all little things he did were important. We had learned the year before in the cup semi when Cooke kicked us to death and that was a lesson we heeded."

The game had been nip and tuck up to a few minutes before half-time when Leon Pryce introduced himself to the proceedings with devastating effect. It was a game breaker.

"It was an innocuous play – a Leon show and go and he just finished it like he could, it was very timely just before half-time which gives you a huge psychological advantage.

"The try just before half-time was less important for us but for them it was a real kick in the teeth because it really deflated them. And then it became a case of next try wins for us. I think that is how Hull felt. As a team then we were good at sniffing blood. It was case of foot on the throat time and we were good at being ruthless. There was no let up after two quick tries after the break," the full back added.

Wellens really caught the eye with his defence, with tackles on the line on Motu Tony and Richard Horne stopping certain scores. The last line of the Saints defence had his own philosophy on keeping the line intact: "The way I looked at it, these guys in front don't miss many tackles here so when they do the least I can do is actually mop up a bit. Invariably that year I did do.

"Those two tackles – on Tony and Horne – were key at the time even though we would have still gone on to win, it kind of said to them 'no chance'.

"What we had that year was a huge appreciation of what each other did. Guys would say well done, good tackle. We understood what each other was giving and I don't think that can be underestimated in any team environment. All successful teams have an appreciation of what others are doing."

25

Daniel's Reflection

"In 2006 we sensed it," said Daniel Anderson, reviewing the Grand Slam-winning season some seven years later during a brief return to England on 2013 World Cup duty for the NRL referees.

Catching up with him at the Griffin, Eccleston, which was his temporary home for the tournament – and a stone's throw from the home he occupied during three and a half happy years in St Helens – he still speaks with real affection for the town and the club.

But he recalls with such crystal clarity the year that he puts up there as his best as a professional.

He continued: "We were very disappointed with way 2005 had finished –but we knew why with the major injuries to key players. We performed brilliantly in the play-offs and had no right to get as close as we did to the Grand Final, but it didn't happen.

"We knew at the start off 2006 we had a few blokes who were injured and could not do representative duty. I spoke to David Waite and told him that if James Roby and James Graham were left out of the England side we would pack the training into them and make them better players. He saw the value in that and did not play them – and that is what happened. At the start of 2006, we had a crackerjack team and we knew it too.

"My first off-season allowed me to stamp my own personality on that team. Credit has to go to Eamonn McManus, too, in that he allowed us to acquire Francis Meli, Jason Cayless and Leon Pryce. The chairman was very good and supportive – he had to be. I am not a revenue raiser, Eamonn had to drive that component of it. He was very supportive and as a coach that is all you want. They were three massive signings and in general the boys at St Helens were already a top class unit.

"But to get three blokes, who were all big, tall players, was a bonus. Physically we got a 103k winger in Francis, who ended up playing eight years here, a front rower who was one of the world's best and a real rare talent in the British game. That allowed us a lot of flexibility in the way we could prepare for 2006.

"I had watched enough tape of Leon – and done my due diligence on him so when Eamonn said he was available I had seen enough of him to say 'I have got to back myself as a coach in this area.'

"I saw him as a fit for the team at stand-off and knew he would be an asset. It helps when players want to change their style. He did not want to be a winger, or a full back, he wanted to be a number six. We had a definite hole in that area for a genuine stand off and even though he was not a genuine six in those days I had watched enough of him to make a tremendous go of it.

"All I could do was make my own decision. He was allowed to literally play at his own pace and introduce himself when he felt like it because we had quality decision makers and structured type players – like Longy, Keiron and Wello. They would always be in the correct position while Leon could float and interject himself into the game when he felt he could have the biggest impact. His intervention just before half-time in the Grand Final epitomised that."

A team of big characters and potentially including some massive egos, plus one with groups of players from different countries – and Yorkshire – there was always a potential for cliques and camps to develop. That it didn't happen was down to the players themselves, particularly the senior ones who set down the rules.

"Our senior players had a key role in stopping any cliques," Anderson said.

"The Yorkshire crew, Baloo, Nick Fozzard, Gilly and Leon all drove across together and if there was a Yorkshire-Lancashire banter, it was just that, banter.

"It was still Scully, Longy and Keiron – and to a lesser extent Wello – who made sure that we functioned as a team. The last voice the players heard before going out on to the field was nearly always Longy's – he was our biggest talker."

The coach reserved special praise for full back Wellens, who was in his absolute pomp in 2006 – as shown by him collecting the Man of Steel, Player of the Year and Harry Sunderland Awards.

"Wello was pretty intelligent and he had lots of positive things to say. Once again, he was the runner and invariably where both he and Longy went is where we prospered because they would make it an imbalance.

"Wello slaughtered all the individual awards that year and prospered from being able to concentrate on his own game. He is a great player. He is a good fella but he was a great player and he deserved that year."

Saints back rower Jon Wilkin described Anderson's strategy that year as "devising a curriculum" for the players to work to.

"This is my style as a coach. I am fairly pedantic on the basics and the techniques but did not see the necessity to give a grand plan because we had too many good players. As long as I just continually fashioned and smoothed out the edges on their absolute basics I was very confident that we had the class to exploit other teams but we needed to do the basics well – that is all I worked on, the basics," he said.

That season there were big advances for five players – wingman Ade Gardner prospered on the flank, not simply because he was playing outside the supremely gifted centre Jamie Lyon, Maurie Fa'asavalu gave real impact after floating around the fringes of the squad since signing in early 2004, the two young Jameses Roby and Graham earned Great Britain calls and Jon Wilkin stepped it up a notch from being simply a promising young lad.

"As a coach you back yourself and I had watched a lot of games in 2005 and saw how players had a contribution to make to the team. Again, it was their own ability I was just there to facilitate it and guide them through. I guess I gave them the belief, that was the key, for them to do what they did best

"I was happy to see Ade flourish because he is a lovely guy and a valuable member of the team. He was easily coachable and delivered. When you do testing on players jumping or running through hurdles – you could see that he had spring and catching a ball, just like passing is something you need to practise. He had the raw talent, all I did was point him in the right direction."

Although three of those players – Roby, Wilkin, Fa'asavalu – consolidated themselves as key members of the 17, Anderson was not averse to taking them out of the firing line to freshen them up when their performances began to drop below the high benchmark they had set themselves. Anderson never saw it as dropping them – rather it was more thinking about each component of that team still firing on full power on the last day of the season.

"It was not to keep players on their toes – the durability of the season and with us being so successful by being in every competition and every game meant that we played a lot of games. So by necessity you need a squad, not a 17-man team, and we invariably used the squad around injuries and fatigue. But when the big games came so too did the tough decisions I made. And we made them."

Of course that meant seasoned international prop Nick Fozzard and versatile Kiwi Vinnie Anderson were both left out for the two big finals.

Anderson said: "The players that missed out on selection for those finals were not meant to take it well – they were upset but that is the necessary evil of having good squads and being a coach. The head coach has to make decisions – that is why you are there. At no stage did they willingly relinquish their positions – they were international players and valued members of the team. I would not like to think we discarded them, we used them as team members and not everyone got to be in every big game."

The other unfortunate issue Anderson faced was the in-out saga with skipper Sculthorpe, but rather than dwell on it he sought solutions that would benefit the team.

"Due to his injuries I never ever saw the best of Scully, he was only really there for about 25 per cent of the time I was coaching and therefore we had to learn to play without him because of his injury. And because we learned to play without him – we could not then toss it all back out when he came back in. With Scully being the man he is and the team member he was, he fitted into the structures that we operated in when he was not there," he said.

It meant that Jason Hooper took that shirt. He was a player who may not have had the prestige and polish of the club's illustrious skipper, but one who gave everything he had, every time he ran out in the red vee.

"You do need to have different styles of players and Jason did all the donkey work, all the unheralded work that allowed some of our star players to play their roles to their full extent because he covered, if you like, the dirty work. It was not lost on me what Hoops and Mike Bennett could contribute to the team. You look for balance and balance comes in many ways. I loved coaching Benno, Hoops and Vinnie Anderson but at the end of the day I had to make a decision on balance and I had some really explosive players and needed some nitty gritty players to balance that out."

Both were great defenders and that was a quality that would always shove them pretty high up the pecking order in the coach's black book. Anderson fitted his blueprint on how to defend on this Saints team, the team reciprocated by leaving the coach with some tips on how to express themselves with the ball in hand.

He said: "Defence is a big thing for me. I consider myself to be a strong defensive coach but I thought that Saints taught me how to be an attacking coach. I taught them how to defend and I just had systems and confidence in my ability to teach them how to defend. We put systems in place and had a lot of blokes who actually enjoyed it. It was the old classic that if you are praised for scoring tries, you will score tries but if you are praised for stopping tries you will stop tries. We learned to praise each other for stopping tries.

"They did not want to let each other down but that comes from team camaraderie and that is fostered by the trust they had in each other. I also had Wello at the back and he was a great general and in all defensive systems, the best defensive systems invariably have an outstanding full back to marshal it. In defence people are exhausted, not looking and in need of guidance – someone to literally tell them where to go. Wello made big tackles himself but he also challenged everyone and we just got into a good system.

"If they needed to tackle then Willie Talau would hurt people, Francis Meli would, too. Lee Gilmour was a brilliant defender, a seriously quality defender. We had positions on the field where it was not comfortable to go to so opposition teams' attack did not want to go there. That is how it was."

Although Saints had won the Challenge Cup and League Leaders' Shield, the year would have been a resounding failure had they come up short at Old Trafford.

And leading out the team on to the Old Trafford pitch beneath the shower of exploding rockets, Anderson had never looked as tense.

"I was blown away, the noise just lifted me off the ground, it was that big. I was apprehensive, probably because we were easily the best team. That's all that it was. You carry expectations and when you are overwhelming favourites it is sometimes relief more than enjoyment when you get the result," he said.

Taking up Wellens' point that the team had "a confidence bordering on arrogance", Anderson explained: "That's right but that comes through every aspect. It comes through your training, it comes through in your game, your preparation and the way you talk to each other. The stars aligned for us that year.

"The team took advantage of a great roster, great support from front office, good coaches, brilliant players and tremendous support from fans. There are going to be teams that go through history that are remarkable – it is unique and does not happen much and they should be applauded as opposed to compared to what followed. It is the best year that I have been involved with in a professional way, the best team I have ever coached in my career, even though I have enjoyed all the teams I have coached. But you are going to get special teams and special moments. Everyone is going to say 'I remember that year!'

"I loved my time at Saints and you always look fondly back at the memories you have. They are great memories."

26

Putting St Helens on the Map

Great sporting teams are judged on what they do on the pitch, the matches they win, the trophies they lift and the style with which they play the game. Saints' class of 2006 ticked all the right boxes and the plaudits they received were fully deserved.

Saints won the lot – Challenge Cup, League Leaders' Shield and Super League Grand Final. The youngsters even won the Junior Academy Grand Final, with teenage prodigy Kyle Eastmond helping crush Wigan 50-12. As for individual honours Sean Long won his third Lance Todd, while Paul Wellens scooped the Harry Sunderland Award, the coveted Man of Steel and the Players' Player of the Year award, Daniel Anderson was coach of the year while James Roby earned the Young Player of the Year honour.

The honour of BBC Sports Personality Team of the Year, with a Coach of the Year going to Saints boss Daniel Anderson, was a little bit of icing on the cake given it is not often national awards come rugby league's way. It was a big deal, given rugby league is hardly in the glare of the media spotlight week to week, players and teams from the 13-man code have to go that extra mile to even get on the ballot paper of awards like that. When it was put in the hands of the people, in a ballot of Radio Five listeners, Saints won it by a landslide seeing off Europe's Ryder Cup team and Sussex cricket team.

Of course, some people believe democracy is great until the vote goes against them and their perceived logic – and that is not just members of the CIA. Instead of accepting that Saints got their just deserts by lifting the honour in Birmingham in December 2006, a string of sour faced, bitter, ignorant, mean-spirited newspaper correspondents queued up to give that decision and rugby league in general a kicking. Churlishly, others alleged that this was purely the whim of an internet campaign and amounted to some woeful miscarriage of justice.

The simple fact is that despite all the hype the European team received for winning golf's Ryder Cup, more people voted for Saints. Prior to the vote Joe Public had a week to weigh up whether a few days golf in Ireland was a better achievement than a club side that had beaten all before it over the course of a gruelling eight-month season. Had the decision been reached by a bunch of old soaks in a cigar smoke-filled gentlemen's club, then the critics and dissenters may have had cause to argue but this was a democratic vote.

There was probably a little bit of guilt there because Darren Clarke had been hot favourite to win the main SPOTY award. He had plenty of sympathy having tragically lost his wife Heather to cancer – but six weeks later honoured a commitment he made to her by playing in the Ryder Cup. Alas, he was beaten into second place by show jumping royal Zara Phillips. And then had to settle for second in the team award – you don't have to be into Establishment plots to work out which of those victors will cop the backlash. Maybe the main focus should have been on how Welsh boxer Joe Calzaghe had not even made the top three. After all this was a year in which the 'Pride of Wales' had taken his record to 42 wins out of 42 paid bouts when he defeated the previously unbeaten but highly fancied American Jeff Lacy to add the IBF belt to the WBO super middleweight crown he had held for more than eight years.

Saints sent a contingent of players down to the Birmingham NEC to attend the ceremony, which was watched by a crowd of 5,000. Among them were Paul Wellens and Jon Wilkin, who both recall the events of that evening.

Wellens said: "In terms of accolades rugby league rarely gets recognition in the BBC Sports Personality of the Year. I remember on the day going to the awards in Birmingham, we told them that Paul Sculthorpe was ill and said he could not make it. There was almost a panic at the BBC – where is Paul Sculthorpe? It was a message that Scully needed to come. We just did not get it at the time – we were up against Ryder Cup and Sussex and remember being there that everyone thought the Ryder Cup team was getting it. So when our name was read out and said we had won we felt a bit bad. Their captain Ian Woosnam had flown in from America especially for it and he was stomping around thinking 'what is going on, what have I flown back for?'

"It was great for us as a team, the town, the players but also for the rugby league family in that finally we had got some recognition. The way it came was just phenomenal.

"In terms of a team of the year and what that team has to do and achieve who could say why were we not team of the year? We performed better and most consistently than any team that year."

Back rower Wilkin is now an old hand at BBC events, but looking back at that time and the awards night itself, he makes some telling points about the sacrifice each and every member of that squad had made in that landmark season and gives a bold defence.

He said: "It was the most surreal night of my life. We were asked to go down and could not believe the really high profile teams we were up against – Sussex and especially the Ryder Cup team. There was a clear expectation that the golfers had won. Everyone thought it would be a formality that they would collect the award. Everyone had achieved something so there was mutual respect."

In winning the award Saints became the first rugby league team since Wigan had taken it in 1994, the year in which they had gone to Brisbane and beat the Broncos in their back yard.

"Winning the award was a special moment and showed how dominant we had been in 2006. Nobody had got anywhere near us that year and I am not just saying that. I honestly thought we were 20 or 30 points better than everyone in that comp that year. To lose just four games all season, with the margins of four points or less, less than ten cumulative points in total, well, I just can't see that being beaten," Wilkin added.

"The criticism from some quarters did not take any of the gloss off. We were battling about the issue rugby league faces as a sport. You could not have argued against us performance wise – we were team of the year because we had dominated the opposition in every competition we had played in. Then just to make sure we backed it up with the World Club Challenge win over Brisbane. We could not have done any more in our sport. We were the team of the year – I honestly believe that.

"The Ryder Cup team is a team of sorts and are popular but it's a team that came together for one week of the year and does not compare to the effort – the blood, sweat and tears we put in from the outset. It is not about picking up the cups – it is things like sitting on a rowing machine at 7pm on a Sunday in Ruskin, doing 10,000 metres and being sick in the toilets, knocking each other out in training and breaking bones. That is what teams of the year should be about. It is about sacrifice, and we sacrificed a lot that year for our success and that is why we were team of the year."

It is not always the best barometer but Saints' domination of the season was underlined with the selection of five players in the Super League Dream Team.

Paul Wellens, Jamie Lyon, Sean Long, Keiron Cunningham were always certainties to be named in the squad given their consistently outstanding displays all term. And Jon Wilkin had caught the eye of the voting journalists with some sterling work long before his cup final exploits.

It was the sixth time Cunningham had made the squad – but had substitutes been selected, his understudy James Roby would have also been a shoe in. The biggest surprise, however, was the omission of all of Saints' props – with Paul Anderson, Jason Cayless and James Graham enjoying tremendous seasons.

On top of the Famous Five in the fictitious Dream Team, there should have been a Magnificent Seven in the Great Britain squad squaring up to the Aussies and Kiwis in the Tri-Nations. Alas James Graham's broken hand injury meant he could not join Paul Wellens, Leon Pryce, Lee Gilmour, Sean Long, Jon Wilkin and James Roby on tour.

Remarkably, Saints' Lions representation would have been even bigger but for skipper Paul Sculthorpe's knee injury and hooker Keiron Cunningham's decision not to tour. There was controversy too, with Ade Gardner, who made his GB debut in that June's one-off Test against the Kiwis, losing his place despite finishing the year with 31 tries.

On top of that two more members of that Saints side of '06 were on Tri-Nations duty with prop forward Jason Cayless recalled to the Kiwi squad and Jamie Lyon's performances forcing the Australian selectors to abandon the unwritten policy of selecting only home based players.

The club's own in-house awards, held at Haydock's Thistle Hotel, saw Wellens take the Player of the Year, with James Graham retaining the young player of the year award. The under 21s honour went to Ian Webster, a player who made his only appearance in the narrow loss to Catalan Dragons.

So the honours had come thick and fast all year – even until the end. But for all the glitter and glamour, coach Daniel Anderson was always ready to 'honour' those unsung heroes whose behind the scenes work made a contribution to the health and well-being of all the club. The way he signed off the last of his weekly columns in the *St Helens Star* that year underlined that commitment.

He stated: "Finally I would like to thank a number of people for their help during the premiership season – Steve Cliffe from Opta Sports Analysis, Graham Jones at David Lloyd's Leisure Centre, Darren Roberts for his weekly Red Bull contribution, Ellison's Coaches – in particular Gary Roughley our regular bus driver, Gavin Wightman at TD Travel, Chris Woodhead and his staff at St Helens Cineworld and Joan's Cosy Cafe for the tasty breakfasts that the players enjoy."

27

Summed Up in a Sentence

Daniel Anderson was asked to sum up the contribution, assets and qualities of the players of his team of all talents in one or two sentences.

1. Paul Wellens – A very intelligent committed player – simple as that. He was the general of our defence.

2. Ade Gardner – He was a rough diamond who really broke out from the footy person he was, into a person who went up to a much higher level.

3. Jamie Lyon – He was just a star, simple as that, and still continues to impress to this day. He was a star then and was unstoppable as a player.

4. Wille Talau – Willie was just a brute and under-rated as an attacking player, but he was extremely capable.

5. Francis Meli – I had history with Francis having coached him at the Warriors. I just loved what he brought to our team. He brought power, speed and personality.

6. Leon Pryce – I was very lucky that I was here at the right time to exploit the brilliant talent that he was. He loved his time here.

7. Sean Long – Longy was basically the best player I have coached.

17. Paul Anderson – Baloo was an outstanding front rower. He

had the hands of a half back and the subtleties of a man who could have worn a number six on his back.

9. Keiron Cunningham – Kez was the soul of the team, along with Wello. They were the engine that drove the team, mentally and spiritually.

10. Jason Cayless – Jase was a tall, lanky, classy front rower who just gave us a whole different perspective.

12. Jon Wilkin – Again I was here at the right time when he exploded as a player and he went from being a good first grader to being an international. He is a very skilful back-rower.

11. Lee Gilmour – Gilly was always in the trenches. He is up there with one of the toughest players I have ever coached.

16. Jason Hooper – Hoops did all the dirty work and made other people comfortable in the team because they knew that Hoops was doing the stuff that they didn't want to do.

14. James Roby – Once again I was here when Robes as a young man showed what was going to be and he provided a fantastic foil for Keiron.

19. James Graham – Jammer became an invaluable member of the squad. I know he came off the bench that year but I don't know if he ever played anything other than first grade from the day I got here.

23. Maurie Fa'asavalu – Who didn't smile when Maurie carried the ball? He was a beast.

15. Mike Bennett – There are players that in their careers go under the radar but they are as valuable as stars. I was pretty confident that I had pegged Benno early as one of those players.

8. Nick Fozzard – Fozz was very entertaining and did a lot of the hard work in that year even though he missed selection in the big games. You need your big men and your blokes at the front to build a platform and he was very good at building a platform.

13. Paul Sculthorpe – My only regret was that I never got to see a fully fit Scully in my time here. The only time I ever saw him at his best was the World Club Challenge against Brisbane where he showed everyone the talent he had and the quality player he was.

18. Vinnie Anderson – Vinnie once again was a very valuable member of the team. Sometimes you can be a victim of your versatility and ability to play a number of positions. And once again he was never out of place wherever he played – a great team member.

28

A Message from the Author

"Are you not thinking of your career?"

The words of the esteemed *Birmingham Mail* head of sport Leon Hickman have rattled around my head on numerous occasions since that day in February 2001 when I handed in my notice at the big circulation, multi-edition city daily to switch rugby codes and head north to my hometown weekly.

As a career move, to an outsider or a bank manager, maybe it didn't stack up, but years like 2006 vindicated my decision to "come home."

As much as I loved most of my 12 years in Brum, there is nothing like writing for your own town, being read by your family, neighbours, and even your former teachers; sure that often means being pulled up in the pub if you get the tone of a report wrong, or edit little Tommy's name out of an under 8s match report, or even being told that 'your' paper lad had broken their letter box, but the pros outweigh the cons.

And some days it is extra special – and it was an absolute privilege to be the *St Helens Star's* sports editor in 2006, reporting on magical days which went on for weeks and then months, putting me in the perfect position to write this book.

What made the job so much more enjoyable was not just the winning – although it is always much easier writing about success – but also the personnel I had to deal with. Despite a team packed with characters and big beasts of the rugby league world, there were no prima donnas in the ranks and all would willingly give you an interview and tell you what they thought. Having to deal almost daily with a real gentleman in head coach Daniel Anderson – a bloke who always took an interest in how you and your family were doing rather than simply what you were going to write about his team – made the task of charting that success more pleasurable. Daniel was a deep-thinking, straightforward and trusting coach to deal with. He was never a smart Alec and if he did not wish to answer a particular question he would never bluster or mislead me, rather simply say: "I won't tell you a lie ..." Most interview sessions invariably ended with him declaring: "Too easy." And at times that year the job seemed exactly that. During Daniel's time at Saints I helped him pen his weekly *St Helens Star* column, interviewing him, transcribing and formatting his responses and sending it off back for him to check and revise. At times it was like waiting for your homework book to return, hoping there was no 'See me' written at the bottom of the document. There again Daniel had transferred his schoolmaster traits into the world of rugby league coaching and made that a real strength.

Professionally and personally the time spanning the 2006 season were the most tumultuous nine months of my life.

The starting point for that journey would have to be press night, four days before Saints were about to kick off their Super League campaign at Harlequins. The paper was jam-packed, anticipation was high at the club and in the town. Jamie Lyon had returned from his winter break to dispel the gloom mongers that he would stay in Oz, and Saints were bolstered further by three new big name recruits. It was a team that was bristling with talent, conviction and a hunger to right the wrongs of the previous season. This was going to be our year – it had to be – and that week's *Star* reflected that.

When I returned home bleary eyed at midnight after sending all my pages to production my wife Kate broke some amazing news – Jason Cayless, Leon Pryce and Francis Meli were not going to be the most significant new arrivals in my life in 2006. We were going to be parents and a quick tot up meant the due date was Grand Final weekend, so even then, four days before Saints had kicked their first ball, I just knew fate meant we would be there at Old Trafford on October 14.

So for me the memories of that journey towards Saints completing the domestic treble will always be so completely intertwined with my family events.

As much as I wanted to broadcast our big news from the rooftops, the plan was to wait for the first scan before telling family and then close friends. Telling my mam she was going to be a grandma for the first time was going to be the Mother's Day present she had craved more than anything, and would more than make up for the day-late bunches of flowers she had endured in years past. That was the plan, but don't they say if you want to make God laugh tell him your plans.

On the morning of Monday, March 6 – some 13 days before Mothers Day – I was laying out my Saints match report page when my dad rang the *Star* office. My dad never telephoned, not if he could avoid it, so deep down I knew it wouldn't be good news.

"Michael?" There was a pause followed by "I've just found your mother ... dead." I didn't hear the rest, but she had suffered a massive heart attack

The reason I have to include this painful bit in what should be a joyous story about Saints' triumphant season is because it was mam more than anybody who fed my rugby habit as a kid and had she not I would have still been getting my sports fix by following the misfortunes of Leeds United.

Sure my dad knows his rugby and can talk Voll, Vinty, Carlton, Boston, Raper and Gasnier with the best of them and can remember where Duggie Greenall 'gave em mammy'. However, it was my mam who first took me to stand on the wall at the top of Dentons Green Lane in 1978 to watch the Saints return from Wembley empty handed for the first time since 1953. Within four months I was a Knowsley Road regular and a year later hooked and a season ticket holder. Smitten and bitten by the Saints bug, through hard times in the early 80s my mam would do without to get me the coach fare for long trips over to Hull KR, or up to Barrow.

So, after that bombshell it was with a heavy heart that I traipsed across to Huddersfield the following Sunday – gazing out of the train window at the undulating scenery crossing the snow-smattered Pennines. That same journey to this day still reminds me of my mam, a Saint who had not seen the team in the flesh since Voll's day but nevertheless still wrote the team's result in her assiduously kept diary every week.

They got a win for her that day and the victories kept coming thick and fast in league and cup, with Saints looking every inch the invincible playing machine. Sure, Saints had enjoyed success before – under McRae, Hanley and Millward – but never the near certainty every week that they were going to win.

All-comers from the so called big four wilted in the face of the high benchmark Saints set – and none crumbled more than old foe Wigan, who up until Stuart Fielden's salary cap busting arrival from Bradford seemed destined for the shame of a second relegation in three decades.

It was hard to believe that only three years previously plenty had predicted that this was it for Saints, that we had won enough and the cycle of success was about to be handed elsewhere. And indeed Leeds would, in turn, dominate the subsequent Grand Final series – but not before Saints had spoilt us rotten one more time.

Nobody was counting any chickens and there was a mighty sigh of relief when Saints won their first final under Daniel Anderson by beating Huddersfield at Twickenham. It was important for the club's well being because Ian Millward's departure the previous spring had been divisive. Had Saints not rediscovered their silver touch then the body of opinion that ditching Millward was a mistake would have festered.

Given the way Saints had utterly dominated the 2006 season one trophy, unlike 2001 and 2004 when Saints had lifted the Challenge Cup and then imploded, was never going to be enough.

As Saints accrued the points during a long, hot summer, my wife uncomfortably carried an increasingly expanding bump – and then with the season reaching its crescendo it was off to Whiston Hospital on the Thursday evening before Grand Final. Thursday turned into Friday and just when it looked like the labour was going to go into Grand Final day, our little Rosa popped her head out late on Friday, 13 October. I couldn't believe how beautiful she was (and still is) although I was never more aware that cutting the cord was the easy bit of the whole process.

After two hours sleep it was back to the hospital on Grand Final day and I should really have waited to come home with the pair of them, instead Kate gave me the nod to dash over to Old Trafford. The game was eight minutes old by the time I had got there just as Gareth Raynor was being bundled into touch, but all the way from the Trafford Park tram station the cacophony of noise was incredible. Gina Coldrick was on the front desk dealing with press accreditation and asked: "What took you?" So I had to explain. In fact I should have explained to all those tense, serious faces all around me in the press box why I spent half the time with a daft smile and the other half yawning.

Saints were commanding that night, but the scoreline is deceptive – it was a tough old game that took some winning.

After watching Sean Long lift the Super League trophy above his head I made a dash for it, but as I left Gina looked across and said: "You will stop smiling one day!"

I was as happy as Larry and when I got home that night I ran upstairs and saw Kate, with tiny Rosa snuggled up in a little moses basket by the side of the bed, I just had to think out loud, "This has got to be as good as it gets,"

Appendix – Saints' Vital Statistics

Games Played 2006

11 Feb Harlequins (A) W16-40. T: Cayless, Wellens, 3, Gardner, Hooper, Lyon. G: Lyon 6. Att: 8,213.

17 Feb Castleford (H) W44-8. T: Gardner, Talau, Meli, Long, Wellens, Fa'asavalu, Graham, Hooper. G: Lyon 6. Att: 13,528.

24 Feb Leeds (H) W13-4 T Gilmour, Meli. G: Lyon 2. Dg: Long. Att:13,443.

3 Mar Warrington (A) W10-18 T: Cunningham, Talau, Gardner. G: Lyon 3. Att: 13,024.

12 Mar Huddersfield (A) W16-18 T: Gardner, Lyon, Fa'asavalu. G: Lyon 3. Att: 8,002.

17 Mar Bradford (H) W38-16 T: Meli 2, Long, Cunningham, Pryce, Gardner 2. G: Lyon 5. Att: 12,352.

24 Mar Hull (A) W0-46. T: Meli 2, Pryce 2, Gardner, Hooper, Lyon, V Anderson. G: Lyon 5, Hooper 2. Att: 11,277.

31 Mar Doncaster (H) CC4 W56-6 T: Wellens 2, Fa'asavalu 2, Cunningham, Long, Gardner, V Anderson, Lyon. Meli. G: Lyon 5, Hardman 3. Att: 6,159.

7 April Harlequins (H) W16-6 T: Gardner, Wellens, Graham. G: Lyon 2. Att: 9,520.

14 April Wigan (H) W48-10 T: Hooper 2, Sculthorpe, Wellens, Long, Gardner, Hardman, Pryce. G: Lyon 8. Att: 17,500.

17 April Catalan (A) W20-34 T: V Anderson 2, Graham, Fa'asavalu,

Wilkin, Long. G: Lyon 8. Att: 8,294.

21 April Salford (A) W10-12 T: Hooper, Hardman. G: Lyon 2. Att: 7,234.

28 April Wakefield (H) W34-8 T: Sculthorpe, Pryce 2, Graham 2, Long. G: Hooper 4, Long. Att: 10,091.

6 May Huddersfield (A) L19-16 T: Talau, Graham. G: Sculthorpe 4. Att: 4,918.

12 May Warrington (H) W34-22 T: Gilmour 2, Gardner 2, V Anderson. G: Lyon 7. Att: 13,250.

20 May Bradford (H) CC5 W42-18 T: Cunningham 2, Wellens, Gilmour, Lyon, Fozzard, Talau. G: Lyon 7. Att: 10,374.

27 May Wigan (A) W14-28 T: Lyon, Meli, Talau, Gardner. G: Lyon 6. Att: 18,358.

3 Jun Catalan (H) CCQF W56-10 T: Gardner 3, P Anderson 2, Long, Wilkin, Pryce, Lyon, V Anderson. G: Lyon 8. Att: 8,319.

8 Jun Hull (H) L26-27 T: Gardner, Fozzard, Wellens, Long, Lyon. G: Lyon 3. Att: 9,907.

16 Jun Bradford (A) L20-18 T: Gardner, Wellens, Gilmour. G: Lyon 3. Att: 12,450.

24 Jun Salford (H) W28-6 T: Lyon 2, Pryce, Wilkin, Sculthorpe, Gardner. G: Lyon 2. Att: 8,307.

2 Jul Wakefield (A) W36-52 T: Wellens 2, V Anderson, Long, Pryce, Lyon, Hooper, Fa'asavalu, Wilkin. G: Lyon 8. Att: 4,927.

7 Jul Catalan (H) W52-26 T: Lyon 2, Gardner, Long, Pryce, Cunningham, Roby, V Anderson, P Anderson. G: Lyon 8. Att: 8,058.

14 Jul Harlequins (H) W30-24 T: Smith, Cunningham, Fozzard, Graham, Gardner. G: Lyon 5. Att: 7,950.

22 Jul Leeds (A) W14-18 T: Gilmour 2, Fa'asavalu. G: Lyon 3. Att: 17,700.

29 Jul Hull KR (Hudds) CCSF W50-0 T: Wilkin 2, Talau 2, Long, V

Anderson, Lyon, Gardner, Wellens. G: Lyon 7. Att: 12,868.

4 Aug Huddersfield (H) W56-8 T: Lyon, Cunningham, Cayless, Graham, V Anderson, Meli, Gardner, Wellens, Wilkin, Fa'asavalu. G: Lyon 6, Sculthorpe 2. Att:8,378.

13 Aug Castleford (A) W4-72 T: Wellens 2, Lyon 2, Long 2, Wilkin, Talau, Sculthorpe, Fa'asavalu, Cayless, Roby. G: Lyon 12. 6,369.

19 Aug Catalan (A) L26-22 T: Moore, Littler, Langley, Ashall. G: Langley 3. Att: 4,551.

26 Aug Huddersfield (CCF) W42-12 T: Wilkin 2, Talau, Long, Fa'asavalu, Lyon, Cayless. G: Lyon 7. Att: 65,187.

1 Sep Wakefield (H) W34-12. T: Gardner 2,Wellens, Lyon, Gilmour, Pryce. G: Lyon 4, Hooper. Att: 8,991.

9 Sep Leeds (H) W54-18. T: Lyon 3, Meli 2, Gardner 2, Wellens 2, Long. G: Lyon 6, P Anderson. Att: 10,024.

17 Sep Warrington (A) W30-38 T: Gardner 2, Wellens 2, Wilkin, Talau, V Anderson. G: Lyon 5. Att: 13,024.

29 Sep Hull (H) QPO (H) W12-8. T: Gardner, Meli. G: Lyon 2. Att: 14,038.

14 Oct Hull GF W4-26 T: Meli, Pryce, Talau, Gardner, Cunningham. G: Lyon 3. Att: 72,582.

Players' Appearances, Tries and Goals

Paul Anderson 26(4), 3t, 1g

Vinnie Anderson 12(15), 11t.

Craig Ashall 1, 1t.

Steve Bannister (1).

Mike Bennett 5(4)

Jason Cayless 29 (1), 4t.

Paul Clough 1(1)

Keiron Cunningham 33(1) 9t.

Maurie Fa'asavalu 1(27) 10t.

Nick Fozzard 11(12), 3t.

Ade Gardner 33,31t.

Lee Gilmour 26(4), 8t.

James Graham 8(22), 8t.

Ian Hardman 8(1), 2t.

Tommy Hodgkinson (1).

Jason Hooper 28, 7t, 7g

Gareth Langley 1, 1t, 3g.

Paul Leyland 1.

Craig Littler 1, 1t.

Sean Long 29, 15t, 1g, 1dg.

Jamie Lyon 32, 22t, 164g.

Dean McGilvray 1.

Francis Meli 27, 13t.

Scott Moore 3(1), 1t.

Leon Pryce 32(2), 12t.

Neil Rigby (1).

James Roby 1(28), 2t.

Paul Sculthorpe 20, 4t, 6g.

Matty Smith 3(2), 1t.

Willie Talau 28, 11t.

Steve Tyrer (1).

Ian Webster 1.

Paul Wellens 33, 22t.

Jon Wilkin 20 (11), 11t.